12 Life Lessons from
St. Thomas Aquinas

KEVIN VOST, PSY.D.

12
LIFE LESSONS
FROM
ST. THOMAS
AQUINAS

TIMELESS SPIRITUAL WISDOM
FOR OUR TURBULENT TIMES

SOPHIA INSTITUTE PRESS
Manchester, New Hampshire

To all who seek to know truth and do good

Whatever is true, whatever is honorable,
whatever is just, whatever is pure,
whatever is lovely, whatever is gracious,
if there is any excellence,
if there is anything worthy of praise,
think about these things.

—Philippians 4:8

Contents

Turbulent Times in Need of Timeless Wisdom

*Help, L*ORD*, for there is no longer any that is godly; for the faithful have vanished from among the sons of men.*

—Psalm 12:1

He who walks with wise men becomes wise.

—Proverbs 13:20

Our Turbulent Times

I strive to write positive, uplifting books that inform and inspire readers with the kind of love of God and His Catholic Church that was restored to me after twenty-five years in the atheistic wilderness, courtesy of the stirrings of the Holy Spirit and the writings of St. Thomas Aquinas. I certainly hope to do the same in this one, but the last thing I want to do is offer haloed-smiley-face Band-Aids to place over the festering sores of our individual souls, of our culture, and, alas, of elements within our holy Church. All times have been turbulent in the two millennia of our Church's history, as the Church consists of sinners seeking holiness, but today the waves of ambiguity and aimlessness, of confusion and chaos, of scandal and secularization, are cresting at all-time highs into a very imperfect storm that puts all our souls at serious risk of spiritual shipwreck. These issues cannot be ignored.

There are all kind of indices of these troubled times within the world at large. You need only turn on your television, your computer, or even your cell phone, to see new examples of turmoil and conflict every day, but alas, such bad news is found not merely outside in the world of the worldly, but *within the very bosom of the Catholic Church.*

The Church in America had suffered and shrunk in so many ways decades before the clerical sexual abuse crisis reared its ugly head again in 2018. Since my childhood in the 1960s, the number of priests has *decreased* by one-third, while the U.S. population *increased* by two-thirds. We have more than 40 percent fewer Catholic schools, while parish after parish proceeds to shut its doors.

We've seen similar catastrophic drops in the numbers of male and female religious. Of those who are left, some remain gallant defenders of the Church, while others gave up the habit of boldly proclaiming unpopular Catholic truths, such as the sanctity of life and of marriage, at the very same time they gave up the habits they wore on their backs, becoming more like social workers or political and economic activists than servants of God seeking the salvation of their souls and of the souls of others.

In Europe, vast numbers of majestic cathedrals sit nearly empty. To the present day, the number of U.S. Catholics has risen pretty much in keeping with our rise in population as a whole, largely due to Catholic immigrants, yet the largest Christian "denomination" in our country comprises "former Catholics."

I came to realize only in the last few years how often during the years of my childhood and adolescence within the Church and my young adult years outside of it that we were told again and again how the Church needed *aggiornamento*, serious changing and updating, to adapt to "modern man" or "contemporary man," to come to "speak our language today" and become "relevant to the complexities of our time." Since my return to the Church in 2004, those winds of change have reached almost gale force, and yet, ironically, those "modern men" (and women) of the '60s and '70s are certainly no longer very modern.

Their winds of change brought us barn-like churches, dislocated tabernacles, and laity-crowded sanctuaries and blew away high altars and altar rails, Latin, chants and bells, and statuary and religious art. It is no pretty thing when the winds of modernist wolves huff and puff and blow through the houses of God, and less pretty still when we breathe them into our souls through ambiguous, novel doctrines that seek to conform the eternal Spirit of the Church to the spirit of the "modern" world.

This deterioration of the Church within my lifetime can give rise within me to feelings of sadness, and even anger at times, prompting me to call out like King David: "Help, LORD, for there is no longer any that is godly; for the faithful have vanished from among the sons of men" (Ps. 12:1). Still, as a Thomist immersed in St. Thomas Aquinas's philosophy, theology, and knowledge of human nature, I remind myself that we are never completely at the mercy of our feelings, even if they appear justified to some extent by external circumstances. God made us in His image with intellects and wills. He gave us both the intellectual capacity to understand the gravity of any problems that we face, and the will to try to make things right, if like David, we ask God for His help. So, although there is no need to be overly pessimistic, even in our turbulent times, we may legitimately ask ourselves where perennial, eternal truths have gone, and where saintly and godly men and women are? Can we *find* them again? Can we *become* them again?

Thankfully, St. Thomas Aquinas reminds us that "the Universal Church cannot err, since she is governed by the Holy Ghost, Who is the Spirit of Truth" (*ST*, II-II, Q. 1, art. 90).[1] The Holy Spirit

---

[1]   I will be citing St. Thomas's great *Summa Theologica* (or *Theologiae*) hundreds of times in these pages. To keep things simple, from here on, I will omit the abbreviation "*ST*" and provide only the part, question, and article numbers cited. For example, "II-II, 1, 90" would indicate that I'm citing the second part of

does not make mistakes because, as Christ told us, "he will guide you into all the truth" (John 16:13). The Holy Spirit does not retire, expire, or resign; rather, as Christ told us, the "Counselor" will "be with you for ever" (John 14:16). The Catholic Church was born on that Pentecost Day when the Holy Spirit descended with tongues of fire upon Peter, our first pope, on our Church's Blessed Mother, and the apostles, the first bishops (Acts 2).

Specifically regarding the papal office handed down through Peter, St. Thomas notes that to the pope belongs:

> authority which is empowered to decide matters of faith finally, so that they may be held by all with unshakeable faith. Now this belongs to the authority of the Sovereign Pontiff, to whom the more difficult questions that arise in the Church are referred. Hence our Lord said to Peter whom he made Sovereign Pontiff (Luke 22:32): "I have prayed for thee," Peter, "that thy faith fail not, and thou, being once converted, confirm thy brethren." The reason of this is that there should be but one faith of the whole Church, according to 1 Corinthians 1:10: "That you all speak the same thing, and that there be no schisms among you": and this could not be secured unless any question of faith that may arise be decided by him who presides over the whole Church, so that the whole Church may hold firmly to his decision." (II-II, 1, 10)

In the recent decades of the Church's decline, we've heard much about "ecumenism" and finding common ground in search

---

the second part of the *Summa*, question 1, article 90. Further, to keep footnotes to a minimum I'll make these citations in the body of the text.

of unity with non-Catholic Christians, and indeed with members of other world religions. Yet, *within* the *one*, holy, Catholic, and apostolic Church we have come to speak of "traditional Catholics," "sedevacantist Catholics," "conservative Catholics," "liberal Catholics," "neo-Catholics," "dissident Catholics," "Vatican II Catholics," and more. Where has the "*one*" faith" of the whole just plain "Catholic" Church gone?

Timeless Spiritual Wisdom

So, where can we go for some of the clearest answers to some of the most important questions about the Faith, questions that bear upon our eternal lives? To quote a previous sovereign pontiff: "Go to Thomas ... to ask from him the food of solid doctrine of which he has an abundance to nourish their souls unto eternal life."[2] St. Thomas Aquinas (1225–1274) is among the very greatest Doctors (i.e., teachers, from the Latin *docere*, "to teach") in the history of the Church.

- Thomas has been known as the "Angelic Doctor" since 1567, when Pope St. Pius V officially declared him a Church Doctor. He earned that "angelic" title for many reasons, as we will elaborate in this book's tenth chapter.
- In honor of the six hundredth anniversary of his canonization, Thomas's writings on the Eucharist, which we'll visit in chapter 12, earned him another sublime title from a Holy Pontiff when, on July 29, 1923, Pope Pius XI declared Thomas the "Eucharistic Doctor" in the encyclical *Studiorum Ducem*.
- On Thomas's feast day in 1999, Pope St. John Paul II called him the "*Doctor Humanitatis*," because he taught

---

[2]   Pope Pius XI, *Studiorum Ducem*, 1923.

so thoroughly about all the good that God has given to the human person, as we will elaborate in several chapters that lie ahead.

• Primarily and foremost, though, is Thomas's most ancient honorific title, given by Pope John XXII in 1323, around the time of Thomas's canonization: the "Common Doctor," the teacher whose philosophy and approach to truth are to be held in common, cherished, and shared, by *all* of the Church *throughout time.*

Almost every pope since that time has heaped praise upon praise upon Thomas, and a main reason is that Thomas's wisdom, like truth itself, is *timeless*. At the time he lived, nearly eight hundred years ago, Thomas was, of course, a "modern man," but he did not write merely for his "contemporary man," but for *us* and for *our descendants* as well. He wrote about fundamental, unchanging truths of God, of the Trinity, of all creation, including man and the angels, and of the Word Incarnate and the Church and the sacraments He left us.

Further, Thomas's genius did not at all lie in novelties or surprises. He always fully heeded St. Paul's words to all the faithful to "stand firm and hold to the traditions which you were taught by us, either by word of mouth or by letter" (2 Thess. 2:15). The Common Doctor did this by preserving, clarifying, synthesizing, and sharing with us the wisdom of the Catholic Church laid down by Christ, the apostles, saints, and Doctors who lived long before his time.

Skim through the pages of the *Summa Theologica* and you will encounter quotations from Sts. Ambrose, Athanasius, Augustine, Cassian, Chrysostom, Gregory the Great, Gregory Nazianzen, Hillary, Jerome, and Church Fathers, Doctors, saints, and theologians of the rest of the alphabet too. Thomas was also well-versed in the strengths and the weaknesses of the greatest pagan philosophers: of Socrates, Plato, Aristotle, Cicero, Seneca, and others, and was literally far more well-versed in the verses of Holy Scripture. You'll see plenty of examples in the pages ahead.

The turbulent world of our times needs Thomas's timeless spiritual wisdom as it never has before. Our Church needs it too, and so do we as individual members of the Mystical Body of Christ. We need to learn to focus on what matters most, to set our hearts, minds, and souls upon God, and to order our lives in accordance with His will as expressed in the two books He wrote for us: the book of nature, which we read with our senses and reason, and the book of revelation, which we grasp in Scripture through the gift of faith.

Inspired by the goodness of God's creation and in humble gratitude for the powerful intellect with which God blessed him, St. Thomas wrote many books from which we could cull countless holy lessons to help lead us not only to better lives on earth but to unspeakable bliss of an eternity spent in the Beatific Vision of God. In these pages, we'll narrow these eternal-life lessons down to a simple twelve, a heavenly dozen that, God willing, will help lead us to Him.

We will peer deeply into the wisdom of the Angelic, Common, Humanitarian, and Eucharistic Doctor and let him show us how, through five "lesson plans" of penetrating fundamental principles of the Faith, pulverizing sin, practicing virtue, praying, and participating in the sacraments, we can live out these eternal-life lessons.

St. Thomas Aquinas is eminently well suited to help us achieve these goals if we are willing to walk with this wise man, listen to his wisdom, and put it into practice in our daily lives. I invite you now to put on your walking shoes and join us in this book's journey.

Accept Only the Best

*Let all the acts of our lives serve
our goal of bliss in heaven with God.*

What is the meaning of life?

Thomas answers that ...

*"The ultimate and principal good of
man is the enjoyment of God."*

—*Summa Theologica* II-II, 23, 7

Goal = Good = God

"What is the meaning of life?" Good question! I was asked this question within the last year for a secular website that has posed it to thousands of people from all over the world, with all sorts of perspectives, and from all walks of life.[3] I won't say I cheated in giving my answer, and I focused on our earthly life for that website, but I must admit that I looked over St. Thomas's answer first! As for Thomas's answer, one encapsulation appears above.

---

[3] You can take a peek at it here, if you'd like: "Dr. Kevin Vost: The Meaning of Life ... and the Virtuous Keys," Excellence Reporter, May 9, 2018, https://excellencereporter. com/2018/05/09/dr-kevin-vost-the-meaning-of-life-and-the-virtuous-keys/. (My debt to St. Thomas, as usual, should be quite evident.)

12 Life Lessons from St. Thomas Aquinas

The ultimate meaning of life, the ultimate fulfillment of why we are here, is to enjoy ultimate and eternal happiness in the Beatific Vision of God. Now let's practice "penetration of principles of the faith" and, with Thomas's help, penetrate further into the profound truths at the heart of this first and ultimate life lesson.

All of us, through our God-given human nature, endowed with intellects and wills, desire to *know* what will make us happy and what we need to *do* to achieve it. Happiness is that ultimate good. If we spend our lives in pursuit of pleasure, or money, or power, or fame, it is because we believe that such things *are* the highest goods, which will make us happy.

Thomas knew well, however, like St. Augustine before him, that our hearts will always be restless unless they rest in God. All manner of human goods — created goods with a small *g*, we could say — are only limited means to the limited ends or small-*g* goals of happiness on earth and will never satisfy us like the ultimate Good with a capital G. Our ultimate Goal, with a capital G, should be the ultimate Good with a capital G, which itself is no limited, earthly, false god, but God with a capital G.

All these capital Gs are the case (uppercase, that is), because God, as our final end, is indeed our ultimate Goal and, as the font, source, and perfection of all that is good, is the ultimate Good. Indeed, Thomas's fourth and fifth proofs of God's existence demonstrate God as the source and perfection of being and the final cause of all that exists (I, 2, 3). Further, Thomas explains God's ultimate goodness in a most awe-inspiring way when he describes how every single marvelous goodness in every single created thing, from the simple beauty of a flower or a baby to the majesty of a mountain or a galaxy, is good because of its participation in the goodness of God:

He produced many and diverse creatures, that what was wanting to one in the representation of divine goodness might be supplied by another. For goodness, which in God is simple and uniform, in creatures is manifold and divided; and hence the whole universe together participates in the divine goodness more perfectly, and represents it better than any simple creature. (I, 47, 1)

So, if you've ever wished upon a star, or wished you could travel to a star to see it in all its majesty (without getting turned into a cinder), or if you've ever wished you could have personally known some great figure in the world's history, bear in mind that God is the source of every single goodness that we admire and that to see Him face-to-face in heaven will so far exceed the combined total of every limited goodness we can imagine that we cannot begin to fathom it. Our hearts are restless because, though the things of creation are good, they are all only partially good and can never totally satisfy. God, and only God, the total and ultimate Good, can completely satisfy our desires, leaving us nowhere else to turn, because through Him we will have it all. In Thomas's words: "It is impossible for one man's will to be directed at the same time to diverse things as last ends.... It is therefore necessary for the last end so to fill man's appetite, that nothing is left besides it for man to desire" (I-II, 1, 6).

So, if we were to recast our question "What is the meaning of life?" as "Good God, what is our ultimate goal in life?" Thomas might answer: "Precisely! By George, I believe you've got it! Good God *is* the Ultimate Goal of our life!" As stated in this chapter's lesson, we were made to *accept only the best*! Let's do our best never to forget it, because this is the lesson of lessons, the "mother of all lessons," we might say for dramatic flair. This is the lesson that provides the "last end" in Thomas's language, wherefrom "we derive our entire rule of life."

So, if we now see the meaning of life, our purpose here, a little more clearly, we have made a little progress in our first lesson plan of *penetrating* to the heart, the principal principle, of the lesson. At your leisure sometime in the future, you can turn to the *Summa Theologica*'s "Treatise on the Last End" (I-II, 1–5), beginning with "Of Man's Last End" and ending with "Of the Attainment of Happiness," to see how Thomas answers a full forty questions in the articles that flesh out the true meaning of life. In the meantime, it's time for us to move on to our next lesson plan of pulverizing sin!

Turning Away from False Goals, False Goods, and False Gods

I imagine that if you are like me, it is one thing to agree that our goal should be the attainment of bliss in heaven with God (and an easy thing to agree on, at that), but quite another thing to live our lives with our eyes fixed on God rather than on *ourselves*. Since the Fall of Adam and Eve, we've all had a battle against sin on our hands. Sin takes our eyes off our heavenly goal and redirects them toward far less worthy things.

St. Thomas wrote that "inordinate self-love is the cause of every sin" (I-II, 77, 4). "Inordinate" means disordered, unrestrained, and inappropriate. It means love of the lower, bodily, animal self over one's spiritual soul; love of simple pleasures, of money, of false gods of every sort in place of love for God. In the terms of our first life lesson, *sin means accepting what is infinitely far less than the best.*

All sins remove our gaze from God and place it on ourselves in one way or another. Lust, for example, has always been very good at tempting us to accept far less than the best. Through *lust* we fixate on people's bodies and remain blind to the souls within them, made in the image and likeness of God. And indeed, while saints and philosophers have historically sought ways to curb lust, it is actively pursued and promoted in our time in ways hardly imagined even but a few decades ago.

Through *gluttony* we live to eat, rather than eating to live. Through *greed* we obsess about obtaining worldly things. Through *anger* we lash out at those who keep us from our sensuous and worldly goals. Through *envy* we are saddened by the thought that others may have more things or more fun than we do. Through *pride* we most directly and deliberately shift our goal from serving God to serving ourselves, doing everything *our way*.

All six of the classic seven deadly sins mentioned above divert us from our ultimate end. We'll look at them in more depth in later chapters for the particular eternal-life lessons each sin most directly opposes. For this chapter though, as I peer over Thomas's broad shoulders, I see him writing about yet one other deadly sin most relevant to our first lesson: "Sloth is not an aversion of the mind from any spiritual good, but from the Divine good, to which the mind is obliged to adhere" (II-II, 35, 3).

Sloth then, is the sin that provides the most direct obstacle to our first life lesson. It takes our minds off the divine good, which is God. This may seem a bit surprising to some. After all, aren't *sloths* those lovable furry creatures that are never in a hurry? Further, in our day, sloth probably first calls to mind "laziness," as can be found in many dictionary definitions. Is slouching on the couch after dinner in front of the TV, dozily munching on chips, truly the thing we must avoid most of all if we are to enjoy life in heaven? Good question!

No, come to think of it—very bad question! We'll have a true grasp of sloth if we understand it through the word St.

Thomas himself used for it—*acedia*, the Latinized version of the Greek word *akedia*, meaning "without," and *cedia* (or *kedia*, if you prefer the Greek) coming from *kedos*, meaning "care" or "concern." The deadly sin of sloth is a *spiritual sloth* that says, "I don't care—about the things of God." Laziness regarding the things of God will also follow, since we are not likely to take much action in service of things that we don't care much about.

Thomas further defines "sloth" as "an oppressive sorrow" and as "a sluggishness of the mind which neglects to do good" (II-II, 35, 1). Sloth is *a spiritual apathy, a sadness or boredom about the divine good of God*. This lack of passion for serving and enjoying God is the antithesis of our first life lesson, and yet it is, in some sense, the first life lesson of the popular culture around us. We can see this in the culture, and within ourselves, when we look at the sins that accompany, serve, and flow from sloth. St. Thomas, borrowing from St. Gregory the Great, notes that each deadly sin has a bevy of "daughters," so let's look now at sloth's sorry brood.

Sloth's daughter running rampant in our culture today is that of "wandering of the mind after unlawful things" (II-II, 35, 4). Thomas agreed with Aristotle that "those who find no joy in spiritual pleasures have recourse to pleasures of the body." In our day of extreme "separation of church and state,"[4] observe how the vast majority of the most heated political debates involve precisely the "pleasures of the body." The most contested hotbed issues of abortion, forced provision of contraceptives, homosexual "marriage," "transgenderism," sexual harassment and abuse scandals, sex trafficking, and legal accessibility to pornography and even to "sex workers" (i.e., prostitutes) now appear in our daily

---

[4]   A political form of the *secularization* we'll examine in this section.

headlines, sparking incredibly divisive debates, marches, protests, lawsuits, and more.

Ironically, too, when Thomas wrote about "unlawful" things, he was referring to moral law, to natural law, based on God's eternal law. The kinds of inappropriate bodily pleasures he wrote against were often "unlawful" in the legal sense too, since governmental bodies realized that legislated laws should reflect the laws of God in order to serve the public good. Even when kings proclaimed their "divine right" to rule, it *bound them* to upholding the *divine laws*, as the Ten Commandments, as instruments of God's will.

Now, so many laws have been passed in the name of pleasures of the body that many of these sins are no longer "unlawful" in the legal sense but have become protected by law and are even actively promoted and enforced on those who morally object to them. Furthermore, the objectors are taxed or compelled as professionals or businessowners to take positive actions to support these once "unlawful" practices. So many minds in our culture have wandered so far toward unlawful pleasures of the body, rejecting God's laws, that it is quite fitting to see this as a worship of *false gods*, and unfortunately, the chief false god appears to be Molech, who relished the sacrifice of innocent children (Lev. 18:21, 20:1-5; 2 Kings 23:10; Jer. 32:35).

Hopefully our minds have not wandered far from spiritual good in pursuit of bodily pleasures, but we still need to examine our consciences to track down and bring home our own wandering, prodigal minds. Spiritual sluggishness is not for the lazy alone. If we become overly obsessed with our work or some hobby or special interest, or even our cell phones or social media accounts, we might be extremely *physically active*, while mired in *spiritual sloth*.

12 Life Lessons from St. Thomas Aquinas

Thomas names other daughters of sloth, including "sluggishness regarding the commandments, faintheartedness regarding spiritual obligations, despair," "spite toward those who lead others to spiritual goods," and outright "malice" (II-II, 35, 4.) It would do us well to see if they lie lurking lazily in our souls.

- *Sluggishness regarding the commandments.* To keep our eyes on the goal of God, we need to ask ourselves if we are doing the specific kinds of things He commanded us all to do, such as honoring His day by going to Mass every Sunday.
- *Faintheartedness regarding spiritual obligations.* Do we give our full effort and attention to spiritual obligations, in things as simple as speaking to God in prayer as well as in things as difficult as publicly standing up for the right to life?
- *Despair.* Are we spiritually apathetic and despairing because we doubt that God could show forgiveness and mercy to sinners such as ourselves? To do so is to doubt God's loving power and mercy and to accept not the best but the worst as our lot.
- *Spite toward those who lead others to spiritual goods.* Have we been spiteful to those who stand up boldly to do God's will? Have we disparaged the priest who dares to give powerful sermons on controversial topics or our neighbors in the pew who are willing to take a public stand to pray at an abortion center and offer counsel to women in crisis?
- *Malice.* Hopefully we do not openly detest the spiritual goods of God, as do some of the most virulent "new atheists" who describe a Christian upbringing as child abuse, but do we do anything to defend the Faith when it is attacked in our presence?

If sloth or any of its sinful, self-serving daughters have a home in our hearts or are expressed in our deeds, it is time to root them out and pulverize them to dust, because they are keeping us from our ultimate goal, and they might well be hindering our loved ones, too, as they look to us for guidance.

Alas, sloth has other powerful allies that quite directly strive to remove our eyes from the goal of God and bring them down to gaze upon the world. One term for this worldly view that champions sloth in our time is the ideology of "secularism." The word derives from the Latin *saecularis* which means "of an age, or a generation," and it has long referred to "worldliness" in Christian usage. Secularism is a worldview with no place for religion and, therefore, no place for God. Those with a thoroughly secularist worldview will certainly spend no time trying to conquer sin as a first step toward loving God.

The highly influential twentieth-century atheist philosopher Bertrand Russell wrote in 1930 that it is not *sin*, but rather *the sense of sin*, the very notion that it is possible to behave in a way that is contrary to God's will, that leads to man's *un*happiness. Ironically though, while Russell would have us throw the very idea of sin out the window, he included in his book on happiness a chapter on the avoidance of envy.[5] Envy, you see, and as every catechized Catholic knows, is one of the seven deadly *sins* the Church has warned against for millennia! Indeed, it seems that Russell and the Church are on the same page when it comes to the fact that envy is deadly to our happiness. (You'd think a logician would be a little more aware of this self-contradiction, but

---

[5] Bertrand Russell, *The Conquest of Happiness* (New York: W. W. Norton, 1996). Chapter 6 is titled "Envy" and chapter 7, "The Sense of Sin."

his chapter on the sense of sin came *after* his chapter on envy, so maybe he had forgotten about it by then.)

By 1973, the eminent psychiatrist Karl Menninger would come to write the book *Whatever Became of Sin?*, arguing that increasing societal problems, the growing incidence of mental disorders, and increasing unhappiness had resulted from the growth of secularism and the rejection of the concept of sin in modern culture. Four and a half decades have passed since then, and our problems continue to mount, as more and more people seem to flounder, having lost track of the meaning of life. Indeed, the U.S. Centers for Disease Control and Prevention reported in 2018 that from 1999 to 2016, suicide rates have risen significantly in forty-nine states, with more than half of suicide victims in more than half of the states having no known previous mental disorder, making suicide not only a *mental* health but also a general *public* health issue. So powerful is this effect that it has led to a drop in the life expectancy of Americans.[6] It is profoundly sad that growing numbers of people in our time and in our nation cannot find enough meaning in life to keep on living.

Although I hope and pray that every one of my readers still has a zest for life, we might also ask ourselves how a downplaying of the dire importance of sin in acquiescence to the social winds of the times has grown *within the Church herself*, not to mention *within our own souls*. To root out key obstacles that keep us from the enjoyment of God, we must pulverize not only the *sloth* that would turn our *hearts* from God but also the *secularism* that seeks to divert and poison our *minds* and *our Church* as well. When

---

6   Centers for Disease Control and Prevention, "Suicide Rates Rising across the U.S.," CDC, https://www.cdc.gov/media/releases/2018/p0607-suicide-prevention.html.

we refuse to accept sloth into our hearts and secularization into our minds, we ready our souls to accept only the best, the things that lead us to God.

Building a House of Wisdom and Love

Hopefully we've begun to identify and pulverize the sins and false ideas that keep us from our primary goal of eternity with God. Now it's time to hang on to our sin-slashing swords while we reach for tools with our other hand to start building up some virtue through which we can train ourselves to accept only the best. Aristotle, after all, told us that we become builders by building, to emphasize the essential role of *practice* in developing any *arête* (excellence), which we translate as *virtue*. I call the house of our first life lesson a house of wisdom and love because the enjoyment of God is the ultimate lesson, and wisdom and love are the ultimate gifts and virtues that lead us to Him. Further, wisdom has long had a habit of setting up households!

- "Wisdom has built her house, she has set up her seven pillars" (Prov. 9:1).
- "Wisdom builds her house, but folly with her own hand tears it down" (Prov. 14:1).
- "By wisdom a house is built, and by understanding it is established; by knowledge the rooms are filled with all precious and pleasant riches" (Prov. 24:3–4).

Wisdom, Thomas tells us, is the highest of the three "intellectual virtues," which perfect our mind's capacity to comprehend truth. The other two are referenced in our last citation from Proverbs. The virtue of *knowledge* helps us to grasp factual data about the world around us. Also known as the virtue of *science* (*scire* being Latin for "to know"), we can see through the modern enterprise of science how this virtue seeks to grasp causes and effects, to see how things work in the natural world. The virtue of *understanding* perfects our comprehension of principles, such as the general laws of nature that make sense of and explain all kinds of particular causes and effects. *Wisdom*, though, sits at the pinnacle of the edifice of intellectual virtue. Thomas tells us that both knowledge and understanding "depend on wisdom, as obtaining the highest place, and containing beneath itself understanding and science, by judging both of the conclusions of science, and of the principles on which they are based" (I-II, 57, 2).

Philosophy means the *philos* (love) of *sophia* (wisdom), and as wisdom exceeds knowledge, so does the philosophical discipline of metaphysics exceed the natural sciences. It examines what is *meta* (beyond) *phusis* (nature). It seeks the highest of all causes and the principal of all principles, which Aristotle, like St. Thomas Aquinas, called God. Aristotle wrote that it is better to know a little about sublime things than a great deal about trivial things. (He accepted only the best when it came to knowledge!) Indeed, the pagan Aristotle, who lived before Christ, called metaphysics the most "honorable" science and even the "divine" science, because it seeks out the things of God. He notes that "such a science either God alone can have, or God above all others."[7]

Metaphysics is the study of *being* itself, the commonality and underlying foundation of all creatures and phenomena studied by any science. Don't worry, though. I'm not saying that *we* must all become professional philosophical metaphysicians. Aristotle

---

[7] *Metaphysics*, bk. 1, chap. 2, in *The Complete Works of Aristotle: The Revised Oxford Translation*, ed. Jonathan Barnes (Princeton, NJ: Princeton University Press, 1984), 1555.

and Aquinas were the best the world has seen, and Thomas, in particular, is a totally trustworthy guide to the kind of "divine wisdom" we need to achieve the goal of our first life lesson.

St. Thomas knew something, though, about the highest of all forms of wisdom that Aristotle did not. Three centuries after Aristotle's death, the Logos, the Word of God, became man; Wisdom Itself took on flesh and became incarnate (John 1:14). Wisdom Incarnate, the God-man Jesus Christ, promised us a "Spirit" who would guide us to all truth (John 16:13), and that Spirit of Truth came, as promised, on Pentecost (Acts 2). Christ revealed to us that the *one* God whom Aristotle's reason leads to is also *three* Persons: the Father, the Son, and the Holy Spirit. Further, the Holy Trinity gives us access to divine wisdom in a way the wisest of philosophers did not know. This "wisdom from above" (James 3:17) is given to us among the seven gifts of the Holy Spirit, the "spirits" or gifts of wisdom, understanding, counsel, fortitude, knowledge, piety, and fear of the Lord (Isa. 11:2). When we cooperate with these gracious gifts of the Holy Spirit, our virtues come to be governed not merely by our human reason, but by the stirrings of the Holy Spirit. The virtues are the oars with which we row our way up the stream toward heaven, and the gifts are the infinitely more powerful winds beneath our sails, if we are willing to unfurl them.

We'll elaborate on the gifts in life lessons that lie ahead, but for now I will highlight two. Thomas, like other great theologians before him, notes that the order of these gifts as listed in Scripture runs from the highest or greatest to the least or lowest, as they descend from heaven toward man. When arranged from the least to the greatest, they act like a spiritual Jacob's ladder ascending from the earth and reaching unto heaven (Gen. 28:12). Again and again Scripture buttresses this view that, to reach wisdom at the top of the ladder, we must begin with the first rung, fear of the Lord:

- "Behold, the fear of the Lord, that is wisdom" (Job 28:28).
- "The fear of the LORD is the beginning of wisdom (Ps. 111:10; Prov. 9:10).
- "The fear of the LORD is instruction in wisdom" (Prov. 15:33).
- "The fear of the Lord is the beginning of wisdom" (Sir. 1:14).

Note, too, how this corresponds with our own "lesson plans." Once we have *penetrated* the principle that the meaning of life is to attain God, our next step is to *pulverize* the sins and errors that keep us from Him. *That very dread of sin is a manifestation of our fear of the Lord.* At first, we fear to commit sins that would lead God to punish *us*, and as we progress up the spiritual ladder we come to love God so much that we fear to commit sins that would let *Him* down. Thomas calls this the progression from *servile* to *filial* (loving) fear. This fear of sin is the first step up the ladder of the gifts that helps us to attain wisdom, which resides at the very top. The *virtue* of wisdom perfects our *natural*, intellectual life as guided by our reason; the Holy Spirit's *gift* of wisdom perfects our *supernatural*, spiritual life, under the guidance of the Holy Spirit.

Thomas says the *gift* of wisdom, like the *virtue* of wisdom, regards the highest realms of knowledge, but it surpasses the realm of *reason* alone and perfects us in the matters of the truths of *faith*, "to know them in themselves, by a kind of union with them" (II-II, 9, 2). Further, because "wisdom as a gift is more excellent than wisdom as an intellectual virtue, since it attains to God more intimately by a kind of union of the soul with Him, it is able to direct us not only in contemplation, but in action"

(II-II, 45, 3). The gift of wisdom, then, is God's greatest gift to our intellect to help us to attain Him as best as we can on earth and to enjoy His presence forever in heaven. It keeps our eyes on our goal and directs the actions of our daily lives in order to help us reach it.

Thomas tells us, though, that this magnificent gift of wisdom "flows" into our souls through the God-given *theological virtue of charity*. St. Paul tells us of the three theological virtues of faith, hope, and charity (*agape, caritas,* or love) in 1 Corinthians 13. He tells us as well that charity is the greatest among them. To *know* God is to *love* Him. When God graces us with the *charity* that allows us to *love* Him most fully, He graces our minds with gifts such as *wisdom* so that we will come to *know* Him ever more deeply.

Note again, as Thomas said, that "the ultimate and principal good of man is the *enjoyment* of God" (italics added). Thomas defines *joy* itself as the effect or result of the love of charity. When we *seek out* something we love, we experience *desire*, and when we *attain* the object of our love, we rest in the *enjoyment* of it. "Joy is compared to desire as rest to movement" (II-II, 28, 3). When we attain God, our restlessness is ended and our joy is complete. As to this perfect joy and its relationship to wisdom and charity, Thomas notes: "The joy of charity is joy about the Divine wisdom. Now such like joy has no admixture of sorrow, according to Wisdom 8:16: 'Her conversation hath no bitterness'" (II-II, 28, 2).

Wisdom and charity are certainly fundamental to meaningful earthly lives and to eternal lives of beatitude in heaven. To accept these supernatural virtues and gifts is indeed to accept the very best. Let's turn now to our next lesson plan to show the means God has given us to acquire and use them to their fullest.

12 Life Lessons from St. Thomas Aquinas

Lifting Our Hearts and Minds to God

We move now to our fourth lesson plan, the fourth *P*, *Pray*. How can we attain the most rightly coveted gift of wisdom? St. James tells us quite plainly: "If any of you lacks wisdom, let him ask God, who gives to all men generously and without reproaching, and it will be given him" (James 1:5). It could hardly be simpler! Still, James counsels us to ask God with faith and without doubting, lest we be "like a wave on the sea that is driven and tossed by the wind" (1:6). He warns us further about being like a "double-minded man, unstable in all his ways" (1:7). Such a person will not receive anything from God.

Per St. Thomas, prayer is "the raising up of one's mind to God" (II-II, 83, 17), and *asking* God for gifts, as James tells us, is one of the key parts of prayer, that of *supplications* (humble requests) for particular blessings, another being *thanksgivings* for blessings that He has already provided. Wisdom perfects our reason, and Thomas tells us that prayer is "spoken reason" (*oris ratio*) (II-II, 83, 1). Further, we learn new truths from teachers, and in prayer we speak and open ourselves to the lessons of the Teacher with a capital *T*, who is Truth with a capital *T*.[8]

Note, too, James's warnings about doubt and double-mindedness. If we experience *doubt*, the very act of prayer is an act of faith to counter it, and we can also ask God through our prayer

---

[8] Truth from the human perspective is the correspondence between reality and our understanding of it, conformity between thing and thought. Not only do created things conform or correspond to God's thought, but "His act of understanding is the measure and cause of every other being and intellect." Truth does not merely exist *in* God, as it can in us, but "He is truth itself, and the sovereign and first truth" (*ST*, I, 16, 5). For us, thinking does not make it so. For God, it does!

to cure us of any lingering doubts. As for the *double-mindedness* that allows us to be tossed about by winds like waves on the sea, see how this relates to the false views of secularism and the sin of spiritual sloth, so prevalent in our day. When our minds are torn between the "wisdom from above" (James 3:17) and the foolish "wisdom of the world" (1 Cor. 3:19) we are whipped about hither and thither by the winds of popular culture, rather than guided along to our goals through the breathings of the Holy Spirit.

Prayer itself helps us progress in the spiritual life by focusing our sights more clearly on the enjoyment of God. Through prayer we reach up to God and allow Him to reach down to us. Powerful prayer may take the form of spontaneous conversation with God or may be expressed through formal prayers handed down to us through the saints, through the Church, or even directly from Christ. (See Matthew 6:9–15, although I'd wager you already know it.) I'll leave the spontaneous prayer up to you, but here I will suggest a few formal prayers to help us keep focused on our ultimate life lesson.

Not everyone may think of this first little prayer *as a prayer*, even though it, like the Our Father, derives from the words of Christ. I speak of the simple Sign of the Cross. In this prayer, we echo Christ, who told His disciples to baptize people of all nations, "in the name of the Father and of the Son and of the Holy Spirit" (Matt. 28:19). St. Paul has advised us "pray constantly" (1 Thess. 5:17), and this simple prayer and gesture can easily be repeated countless times throughout the day to help keep our hearts and minds on our goal of God.

As for the virtues and the gifts that help us to live lives focused on God, I'll provide a few snippets from a prayer that St. Thomas crafted to ask God for the virtues:

O God,
    all powerful and all-knowing,
    without beginning and without end,
You Who are,
    the source,
    the sustainer,
    and the rewarder of all virtues,
Grant that I may
    abide on the firm ground of faith,
    be sheltered by an impregnable shield of hope,
    and be adorned in the bridal garment of charity. . . .
Plant in me, Lord, all the virtues,
    that I might be
    devout in divine matters,
    discerning in human affairs. . . .
Order me inwardly through a good life,
that I might do
what is right
and what will be
meritorious for me
and a good example for others. . . .
    Amen.[9]

I'll conclude here with the conclusion of Thomas's prayer for the attainment of heaven, the ultimate goal of life lesson 1:

Give me, O Lord my God,
    that life without death,
    and that joy without sorrow

[9]   Robert Anderson and Johann Moser, trans. and eds., *The Aquinas Prayer Book: The Prayers and Hymns of St. Thomas* (Manchester, NH: Sophia Institute Press, 2000), 33; 37–39.

where there is
   the greatest freedom,
   unconfined security,
   delightful happiness,
   happy eternity,
   the vision of truth,
   and praise, O God.
   Amen.[10]

Special Aids to Crush Sin and to
Cultivate the Virtues and Gifts

God is so infinitely generous to us that through the Incarnation
and the Sacrifice of His Son, He has provided us with additional
supernatural aids that not only "take away the defects consequent
on past sins," but "perfect the soul in things pertaining to Divine
Worship" (III, 62, 5). Further,

> Just as the virtues and gifts confer, in addition to grace
> commonly so called, a certain special perfection ordained
> to the powers' proper actions, so does sacramental grace
> confer, over and above grace commonly so called, and
> in addition to the virtues and gifts, a certain Divine as-
> sistance in obtaining the end of the sacrament. It is thus
> that sacramental grace confers something in addition to
> the grace of the virtues and gifts. (III, 62, 2)

Now, sacramental grace is, of course, the stuff of the *seven
sacraments* that the Church teaches and bestows. These sacraments are Baptism, Confirmation, Reconciliation, Matrimony,
Holy Orders, Anointing of the Sick, and, chief among them, the

[10] Ibid, p. 57.

Eucharist. Thomas explains that the sacraments were given to the Church by Christ. Indeed, they "flowed from the side of Christ … hanging on the cross" (III, 64, 2). A sacrament "is defined as being the *sign of a holy thing so far as it makes men holy*" (III, 60, 2). Sacraments are special instruments of God's grace that include a visible, material element, such as the water of Baptism, because "it is part of man's nature to acquire knowledge of the intelligible from the sensible" (III, 60, 4). The water we can see with our eyes signifies the immaterial, spiritual grace we can grasp only with our intellects when transformed by faith.

The sacraments also incorporate and give special power to prayer, since a second element of a sacrament is the use of particular words that signify the Word of God. Indeed, "considered in regard to the cause of the sanctification, which is the Word incarnate; to Whom the sacraments have a certain conformity in that that word is joined to the sensible signs, just as in the mystery of the Incarnation the Word of God is united to the sensible flesh" (III, 60, 6).

Sacraments are necessary for our salvation. Thomas reminds us that Christ told us, "unless a man be born again of water and the Holy Ghost, he cannot enter into the kingdom of God" (John 3:5). This rebirth takes place in the sacrament of Baptism. The words that provide the form of this sacrament come straight from Christ, when He told His disciples to baptize all nations with the words we all memorialize in the aforementioned Sign of the Cross. During the Catholic baptismal rite, the priest, while pouring water over the recipient or immersing the recipient in water three times, proclaims "I baptize you in the name of the Father, and of the Son, and of the Holy Spirit."

The sacraments "effect what they signify" (III, 60, 1), and this is of the utmost importance in relation to our first life lesson.

Thomas calls Baptism the "door of the sacraments" (III, 63, 6). While St. John the Baptist baptized with water, Christ, who is the door (John 10:9), gave us Baptism with the Holy Spirit, which opens for us the door to the Kingdom of God.

We will look at all seven sacraments in the pages ahead and see how, when we *participate* in them, they help perfect us in living each life lesson. For now, we might pause for just a minute, to think that every time we make the Sign of the Cross, we remind ourselves that the heavenly door has been opened to us through God's grace in Baptism. It is up to us to choose whether we will cooperate with His grace, if we will take the hand of Wisdom Incarnate and walk through it to see which room the King of Heaven has prepared for us (John 14:2), each room with a marvelous view of all creation, and of creation's Creator.

LIFE LESSON 1 SUMMA[11]

To accept only the best means that we will strive to keep in mind that the ultimate end, goal, and ordering principle in our lives will be the attainment of eternal bliss with God in heaven. Our goal will be served in our daily lives on earth by our reminding ourselves that only God can remove our restlessness, that we must conquer the deadly sin of spiritual sloth, become immune to the cultural calls toward secularization, strive to grow in the

---

[11] We'll conclude every chapter with a simple summary of the chapter's life lessons. As a nod to St. Thomas, we'll call each summary a "summa," but rest easy: whereas his *Summa Theologica* runs over one and a half million words, our summaries will rarely exceed one or two hundred words.

virtue of charity and the gift of wisdom, pray every day for God's assistance, and embrace with gratitude the graces of all of the sacraments, so that one day we may smile upon God in the unspeakable bliss of the Beatific Vision.

Focus on Things That Matter the Most

Three things we must know to be saved.

Question 2
What must we know to be saved?

Thomas answers that ...

*"Three things are necessary for the salvation of man:
to know what he ought to believe; to know what he
ought to desire; and to know what he ought to do."*

—*Treatise on the Two Commandments of Charity*

The Three Things We Gotta Know: to Believe, to Desire, to Do

If we've retained our first life lesson and have our sights on eternal bliss with God, we need to *focus on the things that matter the most to help us attain that ultimate goal*, and that is the stuff of this second chapter. In our opening quotation Thomas tersely lays out for us the *three things* we've got to know to be saved: what we must *believe*, what we must *desire*, and what we must *do*.[12]

What we must *believe* is expressed most clearly, yet briefly, in the Nicene Creed, which we say at Mass most Sundays, beginning

---

[12] You may refer to the appendix to see the table "Three Things We Must Know to Be Saved" and additional summary tables for material in this and subsequent chapters.

with the words "I believe" in English or "*Credo*" (meaning "I believe," and hence our English word "Creed"), the word that St. Thomas used, and the word that you use as well, if you attend the Latin Mass. In Thomas's treatise on *The Two Commandments of Charity*, he does not elaborate any further on what we are to believe, and I won't do so either—not right now in this section anyway, since the remainder of this book will flesh that out aplenty as we examine and strive to live our lives according to all manner of articles of the Faith!

What we must *desire* is expressed just as succinctly in the Lord's Prayer. This, of course, is the Our Father (*Pater Noster* in Thomas's Latin), the prayer that Christ gave us (Matt. 6:9–13; Luke 11:2–4). In the same treatise on charity we are referencing here, Thomas elaborated no further, since his focus was on what charity bids us to *do*. (Please be aware, though, that Thomas wrote entire homilies explicating the meanings of the words of both the Creed and the Lord's Prayer, and we'll pull insights from them in the chapters ahead.)

What we must *do* was expressed succinctly as "the Law," but Thomas spelled out what is meant by the Law in great detail, so now we will get down to business.

In brief, God created the first humans, Adam and Eve, with a natural light to know right from wrong in terms of what they should or should not do. This awareness of *natural law* lingers in us today. Thomas notes that "no one, for instance, is ignorant that he ought not to do to others what he is unwilling to have done to himself."[13] In our original state before we embraced sin,

---

[13] *Treatise on the Two Commandments of Charity and the Ten Commandments of the Law*, trans. Father Rawes, D.D. (London: Burns and Oats, 1880), 2.

our actions readily followed the dictates of this natural light of understanding. Through Satan's envy and Adam and Eve's prideful disobedience, however, sin and the *law of concupiscence* came into the world, so that, as Adam and Eve rebelled against God, our passions and lower natures gained the capacity to rebel against the natural light of our reason. Thomas cites St. Paul, who stated so well: "I see in my members another law at war with the law of my mind" (Rom. 7:23).

Thankfully, however, God came to our aid to remedy this corruption by giving us *the law of Scripture* through Moses. Through this revelation, humanity came to hate sin, so as to avoid eternal punishment. Thomas notes that "the first reason anyone begins to avoid sin is the thought of the last judgment and hell."[14] This then is a *law of fear*. Indeed, not only is the fear of the Lord the beginning of wisdom, but, "the fear of the Lord driveth out sin" (Ecclus. 1:27, Douay-Rheims).

Jesus Christ brought us the fourth and the highest law of all when He gave us *the law of love*. Loving, filial fear casts out imperfect servile fear of punishment, since, as St. John told us, "perfect love casts out fear" (1 John 4:18). Christ's law of love is the highest of all laws that should reign within our hearts. *It is the law that matters the most* and should guide and perfect the acts of our lives.

Thomas elaborates that Christ's law of love differs from and perfects Moses' law of fear in three essential ways:

1. Whereas the law of fear makes us *slaves*, the law of love makes us *free*, as St. Paul says: "where the Spirit of the Lord is, there is freedom" (2 Cor. 3:17).

---

[14] Ibid., 4.

2. The keepers of the first law were rewarded with *temporal goods*: "If you are willing and obedient, you shall eat the good of the land (Isa.1:19). But the keepers of the new law are promised *heavenly rewards*; for example, in the words of Christ: "If you would enter life, keep the commandments" (Matt. 19:17) and of St. John the Baptist: "Repent, for the kingdom of heaven is at hand" (Matt. 3:2).

3. The yoke of the old law was *heavy* and *burdensome*, as St. Peter said to the Pharisees: "Why do you make trial of God by putting a yoke upon the neck of the disciples which neither our fathers nor we have been able to bear?" (Acts 15:10), but Christ said of His law, "My yoke is easy, and my burden is light" (Matt. 11:30).

We'll move on right now, but note that the lightness of Christ's yoke will be weighed and examined with much more care when we arrive at chapter 5.

Thomas drills down into Christ's law of love even further when he spells out a full ten effects of the law of charity or love, "four things that are to be sought for most earnestly,"[15] as well as "six other effects of charity in the soul."[16]

The first and foremost effect of embracing Christ's law of love is *a profound spiritual transformation*. As the thing loved is found in the heart of the lover, the person who loves God has God in himself, for "he who abides in love abides in God, and God abides in him" (1 John 4:16). Indeed, Thomas notes that

---

[15] Ibid., 23.
[16] Ibid., 27.

"it is the nature of love also to transform the lover into the thing loved."[17] There could not be a more complete transformation!

The second of the fourfold major effects of Christ's law of love is the lover's *faithfulness in keeping the commandments*, both the affirmative commandments that bid us what to do and the prohibitive commandments that bid us what not to do, for Christ said "if a man love me, he will keep my word" (John 14:23).

The third major effect is *confidence in God*, for "we know that in everything God works for good with those who love him" (Rom. 8:28). Moreover, Thomas reminds us, according to our own experience in doing things for those we love dearly, that "things hard and difficult seem easy and pleasant to one who loves."[18]

The fourth of the fundamental effects that flow from Christ's law of love is that "charity leads us to *everlasting life*," the ultimate goal of our first lesson, since "he who does not love remains in death" (1 John 3:14). And not only does charity open the gates of heaven to us, but the greater our love of God is, the greater will be our beatitude in heaven, like that of the Apostles, "who have the first fruits of the Spirit" (Rom. 8:23) because of the greatness of their love.

Let's look very briefly at six other effects of charity St. Thomas describes, since he notes we "must not, however, pass by six other effects of charity in the soul,"[19] and we will flesh them out more fully in the chapters ahead.

1. *Forgiveness* from God flows from the love of charity since, as our first pope wrote, "love covers a multitude of sins" (1 Pet. 4:8), King Solomon declared that "love

---

[17]   Ibid., 24.
[18]   Ibid., 26.
[19]   Ibid., 27.

covers all offenses" (Prov. 10:12), and Christ said of Mary Magdalene, "Her sins, which are many, are forgiven, for she loved much" (Luke 7:47).

2. *Light*. Charity enlightens our hearts, for while without the love of charity "we are wrapped up in darkness" (Job 37:19, Douay-Rheims) and do not know what to do to attain salvation, but "his [God's] "anointing teaches you about everything" (1 John 2:27).

3. *Joy*. We saw in our first chapter how joy is an effect of love, since we rest in joy when we attain what we love. Indeed, Thomas notes that the charity that comes from the love of God "makes man perfect in joy."[20]

4. *Peace* comes from the love of God, because no earthly goods can bring us complete rest and contentment, so as soon as we obtain some coveted thing, we begin to seek out something else. Only God brings complete satisfaction, as we will strive to make clear in our very next chapter.

5. *Dignity* flows from charity, for, although all creation serves God, the love of charity makes us, alone of all creatures on earth, free beings and friends of God: "No longer do I call you servants, for the servant does not know what his master is doing; but I have called you friends, for all that I have heard from my Father I have made known to you" (John 15:15).

6. *Sonship of God*. Not only does charity free us and make us God's friends; it also makes us His own children: "See what love the Father has given us, that we should be called children of God; and so we are" (1 John 3:1).

---

[20] Ibid., 29.

The Angelic Doctor has truly given us a great deal to *penetrate* in this chapter's first section, but be not afraid, for we have the rest of this book to peer deeply into its many implications. To put it in a nutshell for now, *we will focus on what matters most when we focus on what we must believe, desire, and do to be saved, in accord with Christ's law of love.* Next, let's take our first look at the kinds of sins and errors we must *pulverize* so that the many glorious effects of Christ's law of love may pour into and transform our souls.

Three Things We Must Pulverize to Be Saved

If we are to open our hearts fully to Christ's law of love, we must pulverize the sins and errors that have grown in our hearts' chambers through Satan's still lingering and festering law of concupiscence. There are a host of sins and errors that can lead us away from God's love. As Satan's minions said of themselves, we could name them "Legion," "for they are many" (Mark 5:9; Luke 8:30). Here, though, we will focus our attention on but three of their names: the ages-old sins of *curiosity* and *covetousness* and the modern-day false god of *consumerism*.

Vices are the tendencies we build up in ourselves that incline us toward the commission of sins. As virtues are to virtuous deeds, vices are to sins, which are, literally, *vicious* (immoral or sinful) thoughts, desires, words, or deeds. We will start with the vice Thomas called *curiositas* because it diametrically opposes our second lesson of focusing on things that matter the most. *Curiositas* derives from the Latin *cura* (care) and is translated into English pretty straightforwardly as "curiosity." Although, in our day, some describe *curiosity* as a great *virtue*, implying "an inquiring mind," the vice of curiosity means the tendency to care too much for things that don't really matter or for things that are harmful and evil. We saw that Aristotle wrote that it is better to know a little about sublime things than much about trivial things, and St. Thomas agreed. Curiosity focuses too much on learning about trivial things that provide simple excitements and pleasures, at the expense of higher, more important things, such as the articles of the Faith. We need to ask ourselves if our curiosity has us spending far too many hours flitting from one website or social media account to the next, when we should be spending much more time and energy focusing on the things that truly matter the most, such as learning the Faith or discerning the needs of our friends and families.

Covetousness for the things of the world (*avarice* or *greed*, if you prefer), is another vice that draws us away from the things of God by focusing our thoughts, desires, and deeds on the acquisition of material goods, "for where your treasure is, there will your heart be also" (Matt. 6:21). If we are to focus more on what matters most, we must work to pulverize any tendency we might find in our hearts to spend inordinate time and energy devising ways to amass money or the limited goods that money can buy. Do you really need to work overtime again tonight, even if you can probably still see the last half of your son's or your daughter's ball game? Do you really need that new eight-hundred-dollar cell phone that your next-door neighbor just showed you—as he chuckled a bit at your outdated model from last year? Are there other signs of covetousness in your own heart? If so, what are they? And what can you do to start pulverizing them?

While good Catholics have for centuries tried to rein in vicious curiosity and covetousness, through "chastity of the eyes" and examination of one's conscience, in our time, in ways never dreamed of before, we are encouraged by advertising, marketing, and our enormous information and entertainment industries to become ever more curious and ever more covetous, focusing more and more on things that matter less and less. One of the most widespread and powerful false life lessons that encourages this the most is that of *consumerism*, the idea that worldly things and worldly experiences are what will bring us joy. Consumerism strives to keep us so focused on animal, sensory pleasures, that we have little time to reflect that, being made in God's image with intellects and wills, we were made for far higher things. Note well, too, that this erroneous worldview of *consumerism* is not merely the product or goal of any one political or economic system, for the overzealous capitalist who lives only for his financial profit may share much in common with the socialist who so dearly desires to possess the material goods that the capitalist produces, or at least to deprive the capitalist of them. Both kinds of im-moderate hearts beat fastest for the treasures of the earth. When we strive to crush curiosity, covetousness, and consumerism, and focus on the goods of the soul that matter the most, our hearts will beat loudest for the treasures from above.

Three Virtues That Matter Much

The vice of *curiositas* has a much abler and nobler foe in the virtue of *studiositas*, which is precisely the virtue that enables us to maintain our focus on the things that matter the most! Aristotle wrote, and St. Thomas concurred, that all people have by nature a desire to know, and we can see this by the delight we take in the information provided to us by our senses. Such is the natural breeding ground for the vice of curiosity. Yet, when we *practice* the virtue of studiousness through repeated daily training, we *pulverize* both our unrestrained *natural intellectual desire* to know things that are not worth knowing and that are potentially sinful, and our *natural bodily resistance* (laziness) to the focus and diligence we can acquire through prolonged study. We can cultivate this virtue of studiousness by the way we arrange our physical study spaces, by removing or turning off potential distractions, such as unnecessary electronic devices, and by carrying materials worthy of study with us when we can anticipate we will have time to sit and wait somewhere, such as a doctor's office or an airport terminal. We can also set goals for ourselves when we sit down to serious study of the Faith. Who could not spare, for instance, even fifteen minutes every day to study the Bible or other religious materials that will foster the growth of Christ's law of love in our hearts and our minds?

Temperance is another grand virtue that can help us focus on what matters the most. Temperance, also known as self-control or moderation, is one of the four cardinal moral virtues that reins in and regulates our desires for the things that bring us pleasure. Indeed, Thomas lists the virtue of *studiousness* as one of many virtues, including *honesty, sobriety, chastity, modesty,* and *humility,* that work in the service of temperance. And how do we become temperate? Here we call in yet another virtue in temperance's stable of allies, namely, *continence.*

In the language of this chapter's life lesson, let's say you have decided to devote those fifteen minutes every morning to the study of the Bible or of some kind of spiritual writing, so that you may have a greater grasp of what we must *believe, desire,* and *do* to be saved. You arise early in the morning, and armed with a cup of hot coffee, conform your contours to a comfortable chair and reach out for something to read. Behold! There upon the table at your elbow rests volume 1 of Thomas's glorious *Summa Theologica!* Ah, but next to it lies the morning newspaper or some magazine on your special interest. An internal struggle briefly ensues, and, thanks be to God, you ignore the paper or magazine and immerse yourself, for a while, in the *Summa*! That internal struggle, the period of hesitancy during which you weighed your options and selected your newly chosen goal of spiritual reading over your long-held habit of beginning your day immersed in the things of the world, was conquered by your practice of the virtue of *continence*. When you have so firmly established the habit of starting your day with spiritual reading that you *no longer feel any internal struggle*, congratulations, for you have arrived at the virtue of *temperance* full-blown. Please allow St. Thomas to explain it:

> Temperance is far greater than continence, because the good of a virtue derives its praise from that which is in accord with reason. Now the good of reason flourishes more in the temperate man than in the continent man, because in the former even the sensitive appetite is obedient to reason, being tamed by reason so to speak, whereas in the continent man the sensitive appetite strongly resists reason by its evil desire. Hence continence is compared to temperance, as the imperfect to the perfect (II-II, 155, 4).

If we stop to think about it a bit, when we embrace cultural messages of *consumerism*, we do not tame our sensual appetites according to reason, but we rein in our reason in service of our sensual appetites, which, as we saw in our first lesson, can never satisfy us.

Expressing Our Desires in Prayer

We can also reach up to God for His supernatural assistance in helping us focus on what matters the most, so that we may be saved. Thomas, you will recall, said that what we should *desire* in order to be saved was summarized for us by Christ Himself when He gave us the Lord's Prayer (Matt. 6:9–13; Luke 11:2–4).

In his prefatory remarks on this prayer, Thomas states: "Among all prayers the Lord's Prayer stands preeminent, for it excels in the five conditions required in prayer: confidence, rectitude, order, devotion, and humility."[21] Surely, we all know Thomas well enough by now to know that he has precise meanings in mind for each of those conditions.

Sometimes modern spiritual writings denigrate the rote prayers we learned in childhood as superficial formulas most fit for beginners, the kind of spiritual "milk, not solid food" that St. Paul wrote about (1 Cor. 3:2); these prayers include, of course, the Our Father or Lord's Prayer, and the Hail Mary. I agree that such prayers can lack spiritual depth if we learn merely to parrot them with little grasp of the deep meanings expressed in every word. When properly understood though, these prayers, which are derived from Scripture, from the words of an archangel, the Blessed Mother, St. Elizabeth, and even the Word Incarnate, are of unparalleled depth of meaning and beauty of expression. Indeed, we will examine many of Thomas's insights on the phrases, praises, and petitions of the Lord's Prayer as we move through our life lessons in the chapters ahead.

Let's conclude this section on prayer with excerpts of prayers from the *Treatise on the Two Commandments of Charity* added by its English translator, Fr. Rawes, so that we might *pulverize* sins and might always know *what to believe, what to desire,* and *what to do* to be saved:

> O Jesus, let Thy sin-destroying love dwell always in my soul. Thou, in Thy graciousness dost forgive me again and again.

---

[21]   St. Thomas Aquinas, *The Aquinas Catechism: A Simple Explanation of the Catholic Faith by the Church's Greatest Theologian* (Manchester, NH: Sophia Institute Press, 2000), 103.

Give me, dear Lord, true sorrow for my sins. The more that I love thee, the more I must grieve when I offend Thee. (34)

O Lord, lighten my heart with Thine own brightness and the brightness of Thy Spirit, that I may always know what to do, what to believe, and what to desire. Lead me, my Savior, in the right way. Thou art my Judge and my King. Jesus, give me joy in God; and let my soul, loving and longing, rest in Him. (35)

On Believing, Loving, and Participating in the Sacraments

St. Thomas said that what we need to believe to be saved is summarized in the Creed. Among the beliefs you and I express in the Nicene Creed is that of our belief in the "one, holy, catholic, and apostolic Church." Christ said, "You are Peter, and upon this rock I will build my church" (Matt. 16:18), and from Christ and His Church have flowed the seven sacraments. Of particular interest for this life lesson is the sacrament Christ refers to in the very next verse of Matthew's Gospel: "I will give you the keys of the kingdom of heaven, and whatever you bind on earth shall be bound in heaven, and whatever you loose on earth, shall be loosed in heaven." That power of binding and loosing given to Peter and passed on to his successors and the priests they ordain is expressed quite clearly in the sacrament of Confession or Reconciliation—*poenitentia* (Penance), in St. Thomas's words. Indeed, Thomas reminds us that this sacrament is necessary for salvation for any who are in a state of sin, recalling Christ's words: "Unless you repent you will all likewise perish" (Luke 13:3).

In the words of our "lesson plans," the sacrament of penance is the ultimate weapon for *pulverizing* sin, since it draws its limitless powers from the One who completely conquered sin. The word "mortal," used for grave sin, comes from the Latin *mors* (death), and the word "venial," used for less serious sins, comes from *venia* (pardon). *Mortal* sins produce spiritual death and cut us off from God's graces, leading to damnation, and not salvation, if we remain unrepentant. In mortal sin, we deliberately turn away from God in favor of worldly goods. The *Catechism of the Catholic Church* (CCC) explains that for a sin to be considered mortal, three things are required: "Mortal sin is sin whose object is grave matter and which is also committed with full knowledge and deliberate consent" (1857).

Venial sins are smaller moral transgressions regarding less serious matters. Thomas explains that such sins do not involve a deliberate turning away from God, but they do entail an inordinate or inappropriate focus on worldly goods. They do not cut us off from God's grace, but "by venial sins man's affections are clogged so that they are slow in tending towards God" (III, 87, 1). Venial sins cause disorder in our souls but do not destroy them, though they may plant the seeds and help establish vicious habits under which mortal sin can take root.

The good news is that through the sacrament of Penance, both mortal and venial sins are forgiven. Recalling that sacraments entail some kind of *matter* (such as the *water* used in Baptism) and some kind of *form* (the *words* of the rite), Thomas explains that the *matter* of the sacrament of penance "consists in the acts of the penitent, the matter of which acts are the sins over which he grieves, which he confesses, and for which he satisfies. Hence it follows that sins are the remote matter of Penance, as a matter, not for approval, but for detestation, and destruction" (III, 83, 2). As for the *form* of the sacrament of penance, this is the priest's words in the rite, in which, speaking *in persona Christi*, he declares, "I absolve you of your sins in the name of the Father, and of the Son, and of the Holy Spirit. Amen."

Thomas also makes clear the three necessary parts or elements of the sacrament of Penance: *contrition*, *confession*, and *satisfaction*.

> The first requisite on the part of the penitent is the will to atone, and this is done by contrition; the second is that he submit to the judgment of the priest standing in God's place, and this is done in confession; and the third is that he atone according to the decision of God's minister, and this is done in satisfaction. (III, 90, 2)

With those elements in mind, let's take a look at the traditional Act of Contrition that one prays in the confessional after confessing one's sins:

> O my God, I am heartily sorry for having offended Thee, and I detest all my sins because I dread the loss of heaven and the pains of hell, but most of all because they offend Thee, my God, who are all good and deserving of all my love. I firmly resolve, with the help of Thy grace, to confess my sins, to do penance, and to amend my life. Amen.

Do you detect in this prayer not only contrition, but confession and commitment to satisfaction too? Further, do you see expressions of the heavenly goal of our first life lesson, and of servile and filial fear?

It so happens that this question of four articles on "The Parts of Penance in General" is the last question Thomas ever wrote in his unfinished *Summa Theologica*. He ceased to write after a mystical experience of Christ on December 6, 1273. Before his death on March 7, 1274, Christ told Thomas he had written well and asked what He might give him, to which Thomas responded:

"Only You, Lord." Thomas reported to his friend Friar Reginald that all he had written seemed "as straw," after his mystical experience, perhaps a glimpse of the Beatific Vision, to which no words could do justice. We'll examine those experiences in this book's conclusion. For now, please note that the priest who heard Thomas's last confession would report that the Angelic Doctor's own simple sins were like those of a young child.

Moving back to our time and our souls, when we search our consciences for sins we have committed, such as sloth or any of its "daughters," curiosity, or covetousness that we've addressed so far, we must always bear in mind that the sacrament of Penance was given to us through Christ and His Church to free us from the bondage of our sins, and that's what matters most.

LIFE LESSON 2 SUMMA

We focus on what matters most when we attend to what we must know, believe, and do to be saved, particularly in regard to the law of love that Christ gave us. We best hone our ability to sustain our holy focus by striving to crush sins of curiosity, covetousness, and consumerism, by building countervailing virtues of studiousness, continence, and temperance, by praying traditional prayers with a depth of understanding attached to each word, and by embracing the contrition, confession, and satisfaction of the sacrament of Reconciliation, which cleanses us of distracting sins and opens God's floodgates of virtues and graces to carry us back to Him.

No Harmony, No Peace!

We cannot live in peace with others
unless there is peace in our souls.

Question 3
How can we have peace on earth?

Thomas answers that …
"Concord denotes union of appetites among various persons, while peace denotes, in addition to this union, the union of the appetites even in one man."
—*Summa Theologica* II-II, 29, 1

Penetrating the Principles of Peace

As a child of the 1960s, I grew up in the midst of the Vietnam War and the American "peace movement," with circular peace symbols and two-finger peace gestures all over the place. By the end of April 1975, the Vietnam War had ended, but wars around the world have come and gone since then. In more recent times, we sometimes hear chants of: "No justice, no peace!" as people protest against real or perceived injustices and imply the threat that unless their demands are met, their behavior may be anything but peaceful.

Now, to desire peace is indeed a good thing. In fact, St. Thomas, echoing St. Augustine and Dionysius,[22] notes that "all things desire

[22] Author of works including *On the Divine Names* and *The Celestial Hierarchy* and believed in the Middle Ages to be St. Dionysius

peace." But what will truly bring us peace? Is the absence of war a guarantee of peace within our hearts? Will justice itself really do the trick? We will examine justice in some detail in our next life lesson, but I'll note briefly here that justice is primarily of matter of giving everyone his rightful due. So, let's imagine that our nation is not at war and no one has treated you or me unjustly. No one has stolen from us or abrogated any of our rights as citizens. I don't know about you, but at the moment, I do not feel that I am the victim of any particularly significant injustice (setting aside the fact that some of my tax dollars, and those of many others, are used to support causes I vehemently morally oppose). Still, if our nation is not at war and we suffer no injustice from another person, does that mean that we, as individuals, are necessarily truly at peace?

The absence of war and injustice between individuals may denote the "concord" or "union of appetites among various persons," as in the first half of our opening quotation from St. Thomas. In Latin, *con* means "together" and *cordia* means "heart," so people in concord are of one heart in their appetites. Their appetites do not conflict. They do not desire or try to obtain what belongs to each other! Such concord, of course, is a very good thing, but it falls short of peace. The actions of no human being, human institution, or society are sufficient to bring any one of us true peace.

Further, there can be *concord* or unity of desire among criminals who work together for evil ends, but Scripture tells us that

---

the Areopagite converted by St. Paul (Acts 17:34). He is usually referred to now as Pseudo-Dionysius or Pseudo-Denys and is believed to be a late fifth- to early sixth-century Syrian Christian theologian and philosopher who wrote under the name of the famous St. Dionysius. "Areopagite" refers to a rock called the Areopagus ("Ares' rock"), near the acropolis in Athens where St. Paul preached so persuasively.

such people do not attain peace: "'There is no peace,' says the Lord, 'for the wicked'" (Isa. 48:22). "Therefore," says Thomas, "peace is not the same as concord. *I answer that,* Peace includes concord and adds something thereto" (II-II, 29, 1).

That additional something is "the union of appetites even in one man." This is the fundamental principle of peace. *To achieve true peace, we must be of one heart, not only in our relationships with others, but within our own souls.*

If the desires in our souls are conflicted, we are in no position to achieve concord with others. This is why our lesson declares not, "No *justice*, no peace!" but "No *harmony*, no peace!" If we do not attain harmony in our souls, in the workings of our intellects, wills, and appetites, we will not have peace in our hearts, and we will fare very poorly at making peace with others. Justice will not live even in our own hearts when we do not do our own souls justice.

The Wrath of Contumely

It is no easy thing to achieve such inner harmony. Long ago, St. Paul, referred to reverently in St. Thomas's writings as "the Apostle," told us as much: "For I do not do the good I want, but the evil I do not want is what I do. Now if I do what I do not want, it is no longer I that do it, but sin which dwells within me" (Rom. 7:19–20). Sin then, is the source of disharmony within our souls. All manner of sins produce and proceed from such inner conflicts, but for now we will zoom in and attempt to pulverize just one sin that especially destroys our concord with others, while also broadcasting to others the lack of peace in our own souls.

Among the seven deadly sins, one champion of discord is clearly that of *wrath*, or excessive anger. Anger can, at times, be an appropriate emotion, prompting us, for example, to take corrective action when someone has harmed someone we love. The appropriate expression of anger must be directed at the right person (a truly guilty party), at the right time (after a delay to allow for cooling and reflection), and for the right reasons (to avenge a true wrong and rightly to punish and correct the guilty party, rather than to harm him). The vice of wrath, on the contrary, leads us to lash out at the wrong people, at the wrong times, for the wrong reasons, and in an excessive manner that brings further harm instead of correction.

St. Thomas, borrowing from Aristotle, St. Gregory of Nyssa, and St. John Damascene, describes three common *varieties* of the vice of wrath that may be displayed by different wrathful people, or at different times, even within the same person.

- *Choleric* people are perpetually irritable and hair-triggered, flying off the handle at the slightest provocation.
- *Sullen* people nurse old wounds, keep them locked inside, and may well come to relish the simmering anger in their hearts as they plan revenge.
- Some are even so *ill-tempered, stern,* or *rancorous* that they refuse to apologize or make amends when they have lashed out in revenge at others, even those closest to them.

If we are to find peace with others, we need to discern when we look in the mirror whether a choleric, sullen, ill-tempered, or rancorous face glares back at us.

Wrath also has several war-mongering daughters who work together in wreaking havoc in our souls and between us and others. One of wrath's daughters is called *swelling of the mind*, in which our calm, rational thinking capacities become overwhelmed by festering, mushrooming thoughts of revenge. Such irrational swelling is fed by *indignation*, in which we enkindle our wrath by mentally belittling the object of our anger. In his ancient book on anger (*De Ira*), from which Thomas sometimes cites, the Stoic philosopher Seneca suggests that one remedy for intense anger is to look at our faces in a mirror when we are enraged to see how insane we look when our mind is irrationally swollen![23]

- A mind and heart swollen with anger can break out in harmful words and deeds. Confused, thoughtless, or vulgar words may burst forth, courtesy of the daughter *clamor*.

- We may purposely insult and revile another person, courtesy of *contumely*.

- Of course, at times some of us may be so carried away with rage that we let loose the daughter *blasphemy*, cursing God Himself.

- Other daughters of wrath sow discord in words and deeds as well, such as the tendency toward *quarrelsomeness*. Some people are always itching for a fight; some call them "aginners" because, although they don't really care what you are for, they are going to speak out "agin" it! At a more serious level, such quarrelsomeness may lead to acts of destruction of property or to physical violence.

---

[23] I cannot help but note here a new related phenomenon, courtesy of modern technology, in which people acting out in public are recorded by cell phone movie cameras and broadcast throughout social media. The incident I saw just this morning involved an individual apparently born with XY chromosomes (a male), wearing makeup and carrying a purse, flying into a harangue of threats and kicking over merchandise when a store clerk apparently addressed this person as "Sir." We need to remember that if we allow wrath to carry us away in public, our image in the mirror could end up all over the world.

12 Life Lessons from St. Thomas Aquinas

Wrath and its daughters are obviously harmful to concord between persons, but they are every bit as inimical to harmony in our *hearts* as well—even our physical hearts! Consider, for example, that modern research on people with the driven, type-A personality indicates that those most prone to heart attacks have a tendency toward frequent bouts of anger. Quite interestingly, nearly eight hundred years ago, St. Thomas wrote that some consider anger "a kindling of blood around the heart" (I-II, 22, 2).

The dangers of wrath have been known to humanity since the Fall of Adam and Eve in the Garden of Eden. Indeed, through envy and wrath, their second son, Abel, was slain by their first-born, Cain. Concord and peace had indeed reigned in that garden until sin entered the world, through the envy of Satan and the pride of man. Ironically, in our time, *wrath* itself is sometimes *encouraged* by people who are not at all religious, but who believe that we can build a veritable Garden of Eden on earth.

The belief I refer to can be called *utopianism*, and it holds that we human beings are capable, through our own powers, of creating a perfect state and society. According to this increasingly widely held belief, once such a state is achieved through some kind of ideal political and economic system, everyone will live happily and peacefully ever after, just as in a fairy tale. In the absence of an actualized utopia, according to this view, we are right to express our wrath toward anyone who we believe prevents us from reshaping the world to match our desires, and to seek revenge for wrongs done by less enlightened people who lived long ago.

Utopianism carries with it not only heinous pride, but a completely unrealistic view of human nature and the denial of the potential for sin in every one of us. It is imbued as well with what psychologists call an "external locus of control," the belief that

60

one's successes and failures, one's sense of happiness and tranquility, are determined by forces outside of one's control. According to this view, if we are unhappy, the responsibility lies not within ourselves, but within our society.

We see a corollary in our time in what is sometimes called a *culture of victimhood*, which sees the world as divided between victims and oppressors, where victims are completely innocent and oppressors start each day by thinking up schemes for keeping their victims down. This is not to deny or downplay actual victims of various specific crimes or abuse, but according to this mind-set, if any of us are not happy and at peace, we need to pick up the banner of victimhood and find some class of oppressors to blame. This view imputes evil motives to those with other opinions in search of "micro-aggressions" hidden within ostensibly benign statements or even facial expressions, fabricating apparent discord in the face of intended concord! This kind of vitriolic nonsense saturates our politics and media today and makes it harder than ever to build concord of appetites between different people, let alone the harmony of appetites within our hearts, the kind of harmony true peace requires.

But what does it mean to obtain the union of appetites within ourselves? How do we achieve it? Is *peace* itself a *virtue* we must build in our souls? St. Thomas answers our last question with a perhaps surprising, "No!" Let's turn now to flesh out each of his answers so that we may more fully understand that without internal harmony, there can be no peace.

Another Succulent Fruit of the Virtue of Charity

Our appetites are in union in our own souls when our passions, intellects, wills, desires, thoughts, and deeds work in harmony to achieve our most important goals, the foremost being that of our first life lesson: to attain eternal bliss with God. We achieve harmony and peace when we do not fight within ourselves and succumb to sinful desires that bring us temporary pleasures but alienate us from God and neighbor. We cannot build such peace in our own hearts by our *natural* powers, but God has given us powerful graces that can do so, if we will let Him into our hearts.

Christ told us: "Be at peace with one another" (Mark 9:50), and "Blessed are the peacemakers, for they shall be called the sons of God" (Matt. 5:9). Might *peace* then be a *theological virtue*, a God-given gift of grace? Thomas says no, and here's why. Virtues are *means* to last ends and, as Augustine wrote, *peace is the last end*, in a sense. When we finally attain God, only then will our hearts be fully and eternally at peace. Peace then, is the result or *effect* of a virtue, the highest of all virtues on which Christ based His law, a law, if you will recall from our last chapter, of *love*, or *charity*.

Thomas tells us that *charity causes peace* because charity is the love of God and neighbor. When charity empowers us to act out of love of God and neighbor, our appetites will be in union with the highest and noblest parts of our souls. Peace *in our souls* is an *effect* of charity, and the law of charity commands us to *keep peace with others* as an *act* of charity. Indeed, such peacekeeping is a most meritorious act. Christ places *peacemaking* among the beatitudes, "which are acts of perfect virtue. It is also numbered among the fruits, in so far as it is a final good, having spiritual sweetness" (II-II, 29, 4).[24]

Peace then, like *joy*, is another succulent fruit or effect of the virtue of charity. We experience joy when we obtain the highest

---

[24] See Galatians 5:22–23 for the scriptural list of the fruits of the Holy Spirit.

object of our love, and with that joy comes the peace that ex-presses the end to restlessness. Only when we place the love of God and neighbor above our inappropriate selfish appetites for things such as material goods, property, power, or fame will we achieve the kind of harmony in our hearts and souls that can bring us the inner peace that can help foster peace with our neighbors as well. This requires that we put all kinds of other virtues within charity's service as well; for example, the *temperance*, or self-control, that will moderate our desires for physical goods that belong to others, and the *affability*, or general disposition of friendliness and kindness toward others, that will leave us little time and inclination to think of them as our enemies or oppressors. When imbued with the affability that flows from charity, we will be too busy thinking of ways to love our neighbors as ourselves to comb their every word or action to see if we can find or fabricate something insulting to us.

A Prayer for Peace

We certainly can and should simply ask God in simple, heart-felt words of our own crafting to grant us the peace that comes from harmony within our desires and concord with the desires of our neighbors. Of course, as Catholics, we are also blessed with a two-thousand-year tradition, including a host of marvelous prayers composed by a host of marvelous saints, and we should freely draw upon the holy gifts that such saintly men and women have given us. As for a beautiful prayer for peace between others, let's consider, pray, and act out in our lives St. Francis of Assisi's prayer for peace:

> Lord, make me an instrument of Your peace:
> where there is hatred, let me sow love;

where there is injury, pardon;
where there is doubt, faith;
where there is despair, hope;
where there is darkness, light;
where there is sadness, joy.

O Divine Master, grant that I may not so much seek
to be consoled as to console,
to be understood as to understand,
to be loved as to love.
For it is in giving that we receive,
it is in pardoning that we are pardoned,
and it is in dying that we are born to eternal life.
Amen.

So dear was peace to St. Francis that a classic Franciscan greeting still used today is "Pax et bonum!" (Peace and goodness [be with you]).

As for a simple prayer for the inward peace of internal harmony, behold the simple, beautiful words of a prayer of St. Frances Xavier Cabrini:

Fortify me with the grace of Your Holy Spirit and give Your peace to my soul that I may be free from all needless anxiety, solicitude, and worry. Help me to desire always that which is pleasing and acceptable to You so that Your will may be my will.

Note well that Mother Cabrini (1850–1917) was the founder of the Missionary Sisters of the Sacred Heart of Jesus.

Let's recall as well the Angelic Doctor's lesson on prayer from our last chapter. The prayer Christ gave us is the model of perfection in its confidence, rectitude, order, devoutness, and humility.

Through the Lord's Prayer, we have indeed been instructed to seek concord with others, as is clearly seen in its fifth petition: "forgive us our trespasses, as we forgive those who trespass against us." Thomas highlights that God's forgiveness of our sins is a great source of hope because of His great mercy, and yet, of all of the prayer's petitions, only this one is expressly conditional. Something essential is required of *us*. We must also forgive those who have sinned against us if we are to receive God's forgiveness. If we pray this prayer with sincerity, we cannot remain sullen and angry with others, seeing them as potential enemies: "Anger and wrath, these also are abominations, and the sinful man will possess them. He that takes vengeance will suffer from the Lord, and he will firmly establish his sins. Forgive your neighbor the wrong he has done, and then your sins will be pardoned when you pray" (Sir. 27:30; 28:1–2).

Still, keeping this prayer's perfect order in mind, before this request for and pledge of forgiveness comes the third petition, in which we pray: "Thy will be done, on earth as it is in heaven." This is our prayer for the internal *harmony* of appetites necessary for true peace. Among Thomas's many insights regarding this petition, he observes: "God wills that man be restored to the state and dignity in which the first man was created, which was so great that his spirit and soul experienced no rebellion on the part of his flesh and sensuality."[25] Thomas harks back to St. Paul's writings on the war between the spirit and the flesh, which will ultimately be won only in the next life, when we are raised in an incorruptible and imperishable state (see 1 Cor. 15:42-43). Even in this life, though, the extent to which we can unify our wills with the will of God will be the extent to which

---

[25] *Aquinas Catechism*, 133.

we attain the inner harmony of peace. Indeed, St. Thomas, in his prayer "For Ordering a Life Wisely," would ask that his own heart be unified in its appetites according to God's will:

Give to me, O Lord, God,
> a watchful heart
>> which no capricious thought can
>> lure away from You.

Give to me
> a noble heart
>> which no unworthy desire can debase.

Give to me
> a resolute heart
>> which no evil intention can divert

Give to me
> a stalwart heart
>> which no tribulation can overcome.

Give to me
> a temperate heart
>> which no violent passion can enslave.[26]

Sacramental Signs of Peace

That Christ wants us to have peace is seen clearly in how He employed an ancient Jewish greeting: "Peace be with you!" (Luke 24:36; John 20:21; 20:26). Each of the sacraments He left us can, in its own way, contribute to peace with others and peace in our hearts. Through the sacrament of Baptism, we all become part of the Mystical Body of Christ, and brothers and sisters in God's family, through the graces breathed into our souls through the

---

[26] Anderson and Moser, *Aquinas Prayer Book*, 11.

Holy Spirit. As we reflect on our Baptism "in the name of the Father, and of the Son, and of the Holy Spirit," may it remind us of the utterly complete harmony between the three Persons of the Holy Trinity and inspire us to establish harmony here on earth, being made in the image and likeness of God.

Through the sacrament of Penance, we take concrete actions inspired by the Lord's Prayer, seeking forgiveness of our sins against others, including perhaps our less-than-perfect willingness to forgive the sins that others have committed against us. The very act of going to Confession is also an expression of our willingness to abide by God's will, since He has called us to confess our sins and provided the means for their forgiveness and the reopening of the channels of His grace.

The greatest sacrament of peace within and between human beings is the greatest sacrament of all, in which we become one with the Sacred Heart of Christ and, indeed, in a mystical sense beyond our complete understanding, with His entire Body and Blood, Soul and Divinity. Note well how we prepare for this sacrament of the Eucharist in every Mass with fervent prayers for peace.

In the Novus Ordo Mass, after reciting the Our Father, the priest shares Christ's blessing of peace, and the people exchange words and a gestural sign of peace. In the Traditional Latin Mass, there is no gesture of peace between the people, but the priest proclaims, "*Pax Domini sit semper vobis cum*" (May the peace of the Lord be always with you) as he makes the Sign of the Cross three times.

Go to either the Traditional Latin Mass or the Novus Ordo Mass, and before Communion you will also hear the Agnus Dei (Lamb of God) prayer, the last petition being "*Agnus Dei, qui tollis peccata mundi, dona nobis pacem*" (Lamb of God, who takes away the sins of the world, grant us peace). After the Host is consecrated, the priest turns to the faithful and declares: "*Ecce Agnus Dei: ecce qui tollit peccata mundi*" (Behold the Lamb of God, who takes away the sins of the world.) In elaborating on this prayer at Mass, Thomas says that "the people are prepared by the *Pax*[27] which is given with the words, *Lamb of God*, etc., because this is the sacrament of unity and peace" (III, 83, 4).

The prophets of old also knew well that this Lamb of God, sent to us by the Father for the ultimate sacrifice re-presented at every Mass, would not only take away the sins of the world, but would also provide us with the only true means for peace with others and within ourselves:

> For to us a child is born,
>   to us a son is given;
> and the government will be upon his shoulder,
>   and his name will be called
> "Wonderful Counselor, Mighty God,
>   Everlasting Father, Prince of Peace." (Isa. 9:6)

LIFE LESSON 3 SUMMA

We will never achieve true peace with others unless we strive for harmony in our own hearts and souls by rejecting wrath and the culture of victimhood and seek to temper our worldly desires and reach out to our neighbors in a spirit of love expressed in the simple, friendly warmth of affability extended to all. We can pray to God for this peace in our hearts, with special attention to the prayer that Christ gave us and to His Sacred Heart. We

------

[27] Latin for "peace."

must remember as well that our truest fonts of harmony and peace during our time on earth are found in the Church's sacraments, which bind us together in concord with our neighbors as we harmonize our wills with the will of God.

Justice Begins at Home

*All justice is social, but it must
begin within our own souls.*

Question 4
How can we be just within an unjust society?

Thomas answers that ...
"Justice is a habit, which makes a man capable of doing what is just, and of being just in action and in intention."
—*Summa Theologica* II-II, 58, 1

"Social Justice" – A Redundant Term?

Cries for "social justice" are heard everywhere today, both out-side and inside the Church, and while St. Thomas devotes more than 60 questions and 260 pages in double-column print in the *Summa Theologica* (II-II, Qs. 57–120) to an examination of justice from every angle, you won't find the term in there even once![28]

---

[28] Thomas does write about "social (*politicas*) virtues" in the sense that all human virtues reflect our natures as not only ratio-nal, but social or political animals (I-II, 61, 5). As for current Catholic teaching on the matter, I just did an Internet search on Catholicism and social justice and among the first articles retrieved was one on the United States Conference of Catholic Bishops website titled "Vatican Documents on Social Justice" (http://www.usccb.org/issues-and-action/human-life-and-dignity/vatican-statements-on-social-justice.cfm). Most interestingly, a

Could it be that Thomas never heard of it, living almost eight hundred years ago and all? Well, there is another answer we can find clearly stated in Thomas's writings, for example: "It is proper to justice, as compared with the other virtues, to direct man in his relations with others: because it denotes a kind of equality, as its very name implies" (II-II, 57,1), and "since justice by its name implies equality, it denotes essentially relation to another, for a thing is equal, not to itself, but to another" (II-II, 58, 2).

In other words, *all justice is social* in that it pertains to people's actions relating to other people. Now, the reason I may seem to split hairs on this point is because I believe misunderstandings of justice and "social justice" produce all kinds of hairy problems in our world today. Check out the news any day, and you will find around the world all sorts of conflicting interest groups, led by what are sometimes referred to as "social justice warriors" fervently demanding that *members of various groups* do what *their group* deems to be just. This is not to say that there are not very important broader, societal, political, and economic aspects to justice that are indeed worth fighting for, but it is to say that *we rarely hear of the need for all members of all groups, for all human beings, to be fair and just in all our one-on-one interactions with each other*, regardless of what is going on in our society's institutions.

Even if redundant in a sense, the Church does indeed give us important social teachings under the name of social justice, the gist of which is provided in the *Catechism*:

---

word search revealed only two uses of the phrase "social justice," one in the title and another in a section heading in the bishops' article, with no uses of the phrase in the Vatican excerpts themselves! The term "social justice" is used and explained, however, in the *Catechism of the Catholic Church*, part 3, chapter 2, article 3, as we'll see in the course of this chapter.

Society ensures social justice when it provides the conditions that allow associations or individuals to obtain what is their due, according to their nature and their vocation. Social justice is linked to the common good and the exercise of authority. (1928)

Rest assured that St. Thomas, too, has masterfully addressed issues such as these, for while the exact phrase that would be translated "social justice" does not appear in his writings, he does explain and differentiate between *commutative, distributive, political, legal, general, particular, metaphorical,* and *domestic* justice, not to mention multiple *special virtues* related to justice.[29]

St. Thomas can help disentangle the problems that arise from our modern-day murky understandings of justice, and he can cast the solutions in the form of life lessons that *we* can apply every day in our lives *as we relate to the living, breathing people around us.*

Rendering Justice Its Rightful Due

So what exactly, is *justice?* Borrowing and honing the definition from Aristotle, Thomas declares as follows:

And if anyone might reduce it to the form of a definition, he might say that *justice is a habit whereby a man renders to each one his due by a constant and perpetual will;* and this is about the same definition as given by the Philosopher (*Ethics*, 5.5) who says that *justice is a habit whereby a man is said to be capable of doing just actions in accordance with his choice.* (II-II, 58, 1)

---

[29] See the appendix for tables summarizing all of these forms of justice and its related special virtues.

In another elaboration used in our opening quotation, "justice is a habit which makes a man capable of doing what is just, and of being just in action and in intention." Citing Aristotle's *Nicomachean Ethics* 5.2, Thomas notes that this statement emphasizes both that justice is expressed in *acts* and that it is *exercised* by the powers of the human *will*, informed by the intellect regarding what is *right* or *just*.[30] You may also note that the idea of giving people their "due" appears in summary descriptions of justice in Aristotle, Aquinas, and the *Catechism of the Catholic Church*. Bearing in mind that the very word "justice" is built upon the Latin word meaning *right*, a pithy definition of the gist of justice is "to render to each person his or her rightful due." Rendering such due is something we are all called to do every day of our lives, regardless of how just or unjust we consider our government or other institutions to be.

To give St. Thomas *his* rightful due in summarizing his life lessons on justice, it is essential that we look at what he called the *virtue* of justice. Recall that Thomas, like Aristotle, notes that virtues are essentially *good* habits—tendencies or dispositions to act in the right way that we gradually develop within ourselves over time through repeated practice. That is why they repeatedly define justice as a "habit." So what kind of habits can we build within ourselves so that we might grow in the virtue of *justice?* Well, I think the best approach to analyzing the virtue of

[30] Thomas starts his long treatment of justice with a question of four articles "Of Right," Q. 57, noting that the object of justice is what is right—the very word "justice" in Latin, *iustitia*, deriving from the Latin *jus* or *ius*, meaning "right." Our American Declaration of Independence speaks of fundamental, natural, "inalienable rights endowed by Our Creator," of "life, liberty, and the pursuit of happiness."

justice is to break it down into "parts," because that is the very meaning of the word *analysis*, and because this is precisely the approach that St. Thomas took.

Now, since this chapter's life lesson is centered on the *virtue* of justice, to penetrate this lesson's principle, we'll change the order of our lesson plans a bit and get to know better just what kinds of *virtues* we are to *practice*, before we consider the *sins* we must *pulverize*. So, without further ado, let's allow St. Thomas to pull the virtue of justice apart and then put it back together in a way that will inspire and equip every one of us to practice it fully in all of its aspects every day of our lives.

On Keeping All the Parts of Justice in Stock

When Thomas addresses the four cardinal moral virtues of prudence, justice, fortitude, and temperance, he stresses that each virtue is made complete by three *kinds* of parts:

- *Integral parts.* The first kind, *integral* parts, are "the conditions the occurrence of which are necessary for virtue" (II-II, 143). In other words, the integral parts are the "must haves" of the virtues. If you lack any one of them, the virtue cannot be fully expressed. Thomas describes them "as wall, roof, and foundation are parts of a house." If it is missing any integral part, the cardinal virtue is incomplete and imperfect.
- *Subjective parts.* The second kind are *subjective* parts, "which are its species; and the species of a virtue have to be differentiated according to difference of matter or object" (II-II, 143). (This will become much clearer when we examine the subjective parts of justice.)
- *Potential parts.* Finally, we have *potential* parts, which Thomas also calls secondary or annexed virtues. "The

potential parts of a virtue are the virtues connected with it, which are directed to certain secondary acts or matters, not having, as it were, the whole power of the principal virtue" (II-II, 48).[31]

Let's look now at the various parts of the virtue of justice.

The integral parts, the foundations of the halls of justice, so to speak, are built upon the fundamental moral principles regarding our interactions with others: "Do the good," and "Do not do evil." The justice of the law courts has traditionally focused primarily on the second, negative principle. We are not to do evil unto others. We are not to deprive others of their rights, or we must pay the penalties prescribed by our community. But the positive aspect of justice is actually the "principal part" per St. Thomas (II-II, 79, 1). This kind of justice was pronounced most fully and succinctly by Jesus Christ, when He gave us the summary of all the commandments — to love God with all our hearts and our neighbors as ourselves — and the Golden Rule — to "do unto others" as we would have them do unto us. For the follower of Christ, then, justice and the love that is charity become closely intertwined, as we seek not only not to hurt our brother, but actively to help him.

The subjective parts of justice are the two primary "species," or subject matters, of justice we've already touched upon earlier in this chapter. *Distributive* justice deals with matters of doing good and avoiding evil that impact entire communities or states. It is most closely related to the realm of "social justice." The

---

[31] St. Thomas uses slightly different wording conveying the same meaning when defining the three kinds of parts in II-II, 48, "Of the Parts of Prudence," and in II-II, 143, "Of the Parts of Temperance, in General."

Catechism notes that *distributive* justice "regulates what the community owes its citizens in proportion to their contributions and needs" (2411). *Commutative* justice "corresponds to the order of one private individual to another" (II-II, 61, 1). This is the "species" of justice at the heart of this chapter's life lesson. Although it is very important to work for a just society, we must always remember that justice must always begin and continue at home. In the words of our *Catechism*: "Without commutative justice, no other form of justice is possible" (2411).

As for the *potential, annexed,* or *related* virtues pertaining to justice, they provide an incredibly rich understanding of just *how* we can *practice* the virtue of justice in our homes and in our societies. So let us begin our inventory of every one of these parts.[32]

Religion

Although it might seem surprising that Thomas includes the virtue of religion among the annexed virtues that fall short of the full virtue of justice, this is because justice entails giving another his rightful due *in equal measure*. Because of the absolute greatness and generosity of God, as the very source and sustainer of our existence, we can never give back to Him *in equal measure* what He has given us. Religion is, nonetheless, "the chief of the moral

---

[32] I should note that when addressing such "parts" or related virtues, Thomas typically forms his whole out of these parts by synthesizing (putting together) previously proffered lists by profound philosophers and theologians, such as Aristotle, Cicero, Seneca, St. Augustine, St. Isidore of Seville, and others, sometimes altering or expanding their lists, and always citing them for their contributions.

virtues" (II-II, 81, 6), and we'll give "the chief" its rightful due, within our powers, when we reach the life lesson in chapter 9.

Piety
The virtues of piety and religion are easily conflated. Mention a pious person and we're likely to think of someone who's religious. Now this is usually pretty accurate. Indeed, God would certainly have us be pious, but there is also a more specific sense of the word. In its most elevated sense as a virtue perfected by a gift of the Holy Spirit of the same name, *piety* honors God, not only as the Creator, but specifically as *Our Father*. Further, per His Ten Commandments (number four to be precise) piety extends to our parents and also to our country (often referred to as a fatherland or motherland in countries throughout the world). In the words of St. Thomas, "man is debtor chiefly to his parents and his country after God. Wherefore just as it belongs to religion to give worship to God, so does it belong to piety, in the second place, to give worship to one's parents and country" (II-II, 101, 1). A proper patriotism or nationalism that does not inherently denigrate other countries is indeed a just virtue.

Observance
St. Thomas tells us that according to Cicero, "it is by observance that we pay worship and honor to those who excel in some way in honor" (II-II, 102, 2). We know that our parents excel us in honor, and all the more so does God. As we've just seen, that's where the virtues of piety and religion come in. But there are many others who excel us in honor, in terms of their excellence or some position of authority they have been granted by their efforts and God's graces. Examples that St. Thomas provides include governing officials, but also commanding officers in the

military, and teachers or professors. We could also include our bosses at work or clergy at church. Indeed, Thomas argues that, in some ways, we all owe observance to each other.

Let's spell this out. There are two main parts to the virtue of observance: *dulia* and *obedience*. Dulia means honor or respect to a person's excellence. To build the virtue of justice, we need to show honor where honor is due. Aristotle tells us that honor is the proper reward of virtue, and Thomas tells us that dulia is shown through word and deeds, by gestures such as bowing or saluting. Thomas states explicitly that *in every other person we can find some quality or talent in which that person's excellence exceeds ours.* Hence, we all owe some measure of the respect and honor of dulia to one another. St. Paul has told us as much: "in humility count others better than yourselves. Let each of you look not only to his own interests, but to the interests of others" (Phil. 2:3–4).

Bending our will to the interests of others leads us to the second part of observance, that of *obedience*. Many today balk at the notion that we should obey others; consider the bumper sticker that says, "Question all authority!" Well, we do need to show obedience to God, and one way we do this is in our obedience to the authority figures placed over us (except, of course, in the (we hope) rare cases in which they would command sinful courses of action). In the words of St. Gregory the Great, by obeying those in authority over us, we "slay our own will" in the spirit of charity. Charity cannot exist without obedience. "He who says 'I know him' but disobeys his commandments is a liar, and the truth is not in him; but whoever keeps his word, in him truly love for God is perfected" (1 John 2:4–5). So, to display both justice and charity, sometimes we must *subdue our own wills* and *question our own authority*, when obedience is rightly due to an individual placed above us with a higher excellence or position than ours.

Gratitude

While religion, piety, and observance render God, our parents, and our nation, those excelling us in some way, their rightful due, the virtue of *gratitude* seeks to repay our debts to all who provide us any kind of benefit. St. Thomas tells us that Cicero rightly placed gratitude as one of the virtues annexed to justice. It was another ancient Roman philosopher, Lucius Annaeus Seneca (4 B.C.–A.D. 65), who literally wrote the book on gratitude (*De Beneficiis*, "On Benefits"). St. Thomas shares liberally from Seneca's silver-tongued words of counsel when analyzing this virtue. I can barely do it justice here, but I'll try to show a little gratitude for what these great men have shared on this subject by introducing just a few highlights and praying that you will seek out more, both in the *Summa* and in the writings of Seneca. "Give thanks in all circumstances," counsels St. Paul (1 Thess. 5:18).

Let us consider the ways to give these thanks. First of all, note that we are to give thanks "in all circumstances." Are you ever tempted to disregard a favor from someone? "Well, she was just nice because she wanted something." "He just gave them to me because he didn't want them himself. Why, everybody knows he can't stand black jelly beans!" Seneca states: "It is the height of malevolence to refuse to recognize a kindness, unless the giver has been the loser thereby." St. Thomas chimes in with his trademark profundity of wisdom and kindness: "It is the mark of a happy disposition to see good rather than evil. Wherefore, if someone has conferred a favor not as he ought have conferred it, the recipient should not for that reason withhold his thanks" (II-II, 106, 3). How, then, do we show our gratitude to our benefactors in all circumstances? Seneca says, "Do you wish to repay a favor? Receive it graciously." Even if we are benefited by someone so rich or powerful that we can never repay him in kind, we can still repay by our attitude, our facial expression, our words, and our deeds, or, as Seneca notes, with "good advice, frequent fellowship, affable and pleasant conversation without flattery." Further, the grateful "outpourings of one' heart" should be heard, not only within the benefactor's earshot, but within the hearing of others, repaying the benefactor with well-earned honor. Aristotle has noted after all, that honor is virtue's reward. The benefactor who receives some well-earned esteem may then be all the more inspired to seek new ways to continue to benefit others.

When benefits are to be repaid, we should do so promptly and gladly, but we should not be in such a hurry to repay that we inconvenience the giver or make him feel as if we have been made uncomfortable by the very favor he conferred. And what then is the height of *ingratitude*? It is not to fail to repay the favor, because we may not always be able to repay, though we would dearly like to. The height of ingratitude is to *forget* the favor or ignore the debt through negligence. Surely we've all sinned through ingratitude at one time or another. But how should the person who displays the virtue of gratitude treat the person who does not? We learn from the Gospel of Luke, "the beloved physician," that Jesus told us "lend, expect nothing in return" (Luke 6:35). Quite fittingly, St. Thomas advises us that "he that bestows a favor must not at once act the part of a punisher of ingratitude, but rather that of a kindly physician, by healing the ingratitude with repeated favors" (II-II, 107, 4).

Vengeance
It may be surprising to see *vengeance* listed as a virtue. Well, some sins are worse than ingratitude and do require a punishment. This is where the virtue of *vindicta*, or vengeance, comes in. Cicero tells us that "by vengeance we resist force, or wrong, and in general,

whatever is obscure (i.e., derogatory), either by self-defense or by avenging it." Vengeance as a virtue entails developing the habit of punishing wrongdoing within the realm of one's rightful authority, and in the spirit of helping the wrongdoer, or at least protecting innocent victims. Per Thomas, "vengeance is lawful and virtuous so far as it tends to the prevention of evil" (II-II, 108, 3). Note, however, that those with the virtue of vengeance will be slow to take vengeance for wrongdoings they themselves receive, "but they do not bear with them so as to endure the wrongs they inflict on God and their neighbor" (II-II, 108, 1). Vengeance must be exercised with great care, and punishment should be delayed while one is angry so it won't be excessive and harm the wrongdoer.

Truth
We owe each other the truth. No one wants to be lied to, and God has instructed us in the eighth commandment not to bear false witness against our neighbor. What we believe or know should correspond to what we say. To tell the truth is a good act. To develop within ourselves the habit of telling the truth, then, is a moral virtue essential to justice.

Friendliness
Thomas explains that the friendliness (*amicitia*) that is called affability (*affabilitas*) is a part of the virtue of justice and something we owe to every person we meet. Not everyone can become a close friend, but because of our social nature, we derive joy from one another's company, and we owe it to one another not to rob others of their joy by our rudeness, neglect, or disrespect. Indeed, "a certain natural equity obliges a man to live agreeably with his fellow-men; unless some reason should oblige him to sadden

them for their good" (II-II, 114, 2).[33] A brief hello or a simple acknowledging nod and a smile are among the simplest ways to display this simple, yet important virtue connected to justice.

Liberality
Liberality means freely giving, deriving from the Latin adjective *liber*, "free." Thomas notes that the virtue of liberality is related to justice, since it involves our dealings with others involving external goods, but "justice gives another what is his, whereas liberality gives another what is one's own" (II-II, 117, 5). Further, justice considers "the legal due," while liberality "considers a certain moral due" (ibid.). Liberality, then, is related to justice, but is, in a sense, a generosity beyond the call of legal duty and of nature. As Thomas puts it so well, "To spend money on oneself is an inclination of nature; hence to spend money on others belongs properly to virtue" (ibid.). We must note as well, that liberality does not imply recklessness in our giving. Thomas uses an apt military metaphor here, noting that a virtuous soldier's fortitude consists not only in wielding his sword in battle, but in sharpening it between battles and storing it in its sheath. So, too, liberality means not only giving away money, but always using reasonable means to earn money and save it, so that it can be employed when it is truly needed.

Pulverizing Injustice in All Its Forms

To grow in the virtue of justice, and its many companion virtues that bring it to perfection, there's a vast and motley batch of vices and sins we must strive to conquer. Since justice relates to all

---

[33] For a look at important cases in which we are obliged to disagree with another for his own good, see the life lesson in chapter 7.

manner of human dealings, unfortunately, there are many forms of injustice, of failing to give another his rightful due — or of outright taking it from him! Among the most serious and blatant injustices Thomas brings up are *theft*, in which we secretly steal money or goods from another; *robbery*, in which we do so openly with force; *adultery*, in which we deprive another of the rightful exclusive intimacy of his or her spouse; and most blatant of all, *murder*, in which we deprive an innocent person of the ultimate right of life. Thankfully, even in our day, most people clearly see the injustices involved in such acts, with the woeful exceptions of the taking of the lives of the unborn through abortion and of the frail, elderly, or disabled through "euthanasia" and "assisted suicide."

We will focus most in this section on the kinds of subtle injustices that we may all commit in the course of our daily lives, the kinds of unjust behaviors that keep us from practicing justice in our homes. One simple way to examine one's own conscience for unjust behaviors is to reflect upon our previous list of the virtues connected to justice to see whether we have, by intention or through neglect, failed to exercise them with those around us. We might ask ourselves if we have been neglectful in contacting or helping out our parents; if we have disrespectfully and unjustly disparaged our nation and the offices of our public officials; if we have been ingrates, unthankful for what God and others have done for us; if we have let serious injustices within our homes go unpunished, or doled out harsh punishments in a cruel manner; if we have been unwelcoming to friends or strangers, untruthful, or stingy with our wealth?

If so, we must formulate concrete plans of specific behaviors we will perform to begin giving others their rightful due. All virtues, by definition (Thomas's and Aristotle's anyway), work to achieve good results *and* help to make the doer good. Virtues also lead to the virtuous person's happiness. So, by growing in the social virtue of justice, we also, metaphorically speaking, do ourselves justice, as well.

To dig a little deeper into the many malicious foes of commutative justice between individuals, let's look at some of the more common sins we may commit that fail to give our neighbor his rightful due. In January 2019, during the national March for Life in Washington, D.C., many news organizations, celebrities, private individuals, and even some Catholic bishops, based on a brief snippet of video footage, disparaged and pronounced judgment on a group of teenage boys for their seemingly unjust behaviors. Many of these jump-the-gun-judges would soon after retract their statements and apologize when further video evidence provided the full story and showed that the boys were not egregious aggressors. Well, nearly eight hundred years ago, in his examination of the virtue of justice, Thomas wrote an ever timely article on "Whether It is Unlawful to Form a Judgment from Suspicion?" (II-II, 60, 3), which warrants extensive quotation:

> Now there are three degrees of suspicion. The first degree is when a man begins to doubt another's goodness from slight indications. This is a venial and a light sin; for *it belongs to human temptation without which no man can go through this life*, according to a gloss on 1 Cor. 4:5, *Judge not before the time*. The second degree is when a man, from slight indications, esteems another man's wickedness as certain. This is a mortal sin if it be about grave matter, since the same gloss goes on to say: *If then we cannot avoid suspicions, because we are human, we must nevertheless*

*restrain our judgment, and refrain from forming a definite and
fixed opinion.* The third degree is when a judge goes so far
as to condemn a man on suspicion; this pertains directly
to injustice, and consequently is a mortal sin. (II-II, 60, 3)

If we are to grow in justice, we must look within ourselves for
thoughts, words, and actions of falsely prejudging others, some
of which could be mortal to our souls. Do we tend to pronounce
people guilty before they've been proven so? Indeed, we might
train ourselves to err, if we must, by giving others the benefit of
the doubt. Hear Thomas again on this one:

He who interprets doubtful behaviors for the best, may
happen to be deceived more often than not; yet it is better to err frequently through thinking well of the wicked
man, than to err less frequently through having an evil
opinion of a good man, because in the latter an injury is
inflicted, but not in the former. (II-II, 60, 4)

Praying for Justice

We are all called to do our part to practice the kinds of just acts
that will help the virtue of justice grow as a habit in our souls.
Aristotle said that we become builders by building and harpists
by playing the harp. So, too, do we become just people by carrying out just acts, again and again and again. Of course, Thomas,
as a Christian, knew something that Aristotle did not. After
God became Man, He gave us an amazing instruction: "Ask,
and it will be given you; seek, and you will find; knock, and it
will be opened to you" (Matt. 7:7). We do not stand alone in
our quest for virtues like justice. God openly invites us to ask
Him for them, to seek them through Him, and to knock on
His door, inside of which they lie waiting for us. We have seen

that He spelled it out clearly for the virtue and gift of wisdom: "If any of you lacks wisdom, let him ask God, who gives to all men generously and without reproaching, and it will be given to him" (James 1:5).

In prayers of petition we ask God to give us what we need to live our lives in accordance with His will. As we strive to live out this chapter's lesson to let justice begin in our homes, we can ask God sincerely and in good faith to help us grow in justice, to become more aware of the simple situations that provide us opportunities to act justly and to share with those around us the shining splendors of justice.[34] We can also let Thomas's analysis of the parts of the virtue of justice guide us in the precision of our petitions for justice. We can ask God to grant us the virtue of justice so that we may always do good and avoid evil, so that we may act justly in our face-to-face dealings with others and in striving to create a society that will deal with all citizens justly, and so that we will be just in our dealings with God, the Church, our parents, our nation, and with everyone we meet through the virtues of religion, piety, observance, gratitude, vengeance, truth, friendliness, and liberality. And speaking of piety, let us also pray that we will be receptive to the Holy Spirit's gift of piety, whereby the virtue of piety is perfected and we treat God as our Father and others as our brothers and sisters in Christ, guided not merely by our reason, but by the stirrings of the Holy Spirit. Finally, speaking of gratitude, let our prayers not only *ask* God

---

[34] In II-II, 58, 12, Thomas cites Cicero: "Justice is the most resplendent of the virtues, and gives its name to a good man"; and he cites Aristotle: "The most excellent of the virtues would seem to be justice, and more glorious than either the evening or the morning star."

for justice, but *thank* Him for his boundless liberality in giving us all so far beyond our due, and pray for all who have shared the fruits of their virtue of justice with us.

More Than Just Sacraments

Every sacrament is more than merely just, exceeding the glory of even justice itself, we might say, as the sun exceeds the glory of the evening or morning star! God gives us so much more than we can ever repay in due measure. He is the source and sustainer of our very being, of every good we possess on earth, and of the ultimate reward of bliss with Him in heaven. Indeed, every sacrament exceeds the equal measures of justice and is a gift of unfathomable liberality designed to help us attain that heavenly goal. Ancient tradition has paired each of the seven sacraments with one of the three theological or four cardinal virtues, and the sacrament paired most specifically with justice is the sacrament of Reconciliation.[35] When we go to Confession, we can make amends for any injustices we have committed against God or neighbor. Indeed, when we review our consciences for violations of the Ten Commandments, we search our memories for thoughts, words, and deeds of injustice toward God in the first three commandments and against our neighbor in commandments four through ten. God stands ready, thankfully, through the instrument of the priest, to forgive all such sins and to supply us with the grace to better resist temptations to all manners of injustice, so that when we go home, we will bring His justice with us.

[35] The pairings were Baptism and faith, Anointing of the Sick and hope, the Eucharist and charity, Holy Orders and prudence, Penance and justice, Confirmation and fortitude, and Matrimony and temperance. Do you see the sense of these wonderful, supernatural correlations?

LIFE LESSON 4 SUMMA

All justice is social in that it relates to our dealings with others, giving to all their rightful due. We can usefully distinguish between *distributive* justice, involving fair dealings within communities and institutions, and *commutative* justice, involving our personal, one-on-one dealings with others. Although we often cannot directly change large institutions, it is up to us whether we deal justly with those in our own lives, and the *Catechism* has made clear that there can be no distributive justice without commutative justice. In simple terms, *justice must begin at home.* St. Thomas has given us invaluable aid in detailing many specific virtues, such as piety, observance, friendliness, gratitude, and more, that we can employ in our daily lives to treat those around us justly. We can pray that God helps us to grow in the beautiful virtue of justice, and we can show Him gratitude for exceeding the bounds of justice in giving us so much more than we could ever earn. This gratitude can also be shown by embracing the sacrament of Reconciliation—the very sacrament of justice (and indeed, of God's mercy).

Our Brothers (and Sisters) Ain't Heavy

Christ's yoke is light when we help each other to carry it.

Are we our brothers' keepers?

Thomas answers that ...

"It is written (Matt 22:39): 'The second commandment is like this: Thou shalt love thy neighbor as thyself.' . . . This precept is fittingly expressed, for it indicates both the reason for loving and the mode of love. . . . Nor does it matter whether we say 'neighbor' or 'brother' according to 1 John 4:21, or 'friend' according to Leviticus 19:18, because all the words express the same affinity."

—*Summa Theologica* II-II, 44, 7

Homini Homo Lupus Est?

Question 5 paraphrases Cain, who answered God's question about his slain brother Abel's whereabouts, "I do not know; am I my brother's keeper?" (Gen. 4:9). The question in this section's heading—meaning "Is man wolf to man?"—is a Latin proverb going back at least to an ancient Roman play by Plautus from the fifth century B.C. The full line reads that a man is like a wolf to a stranger, to a man he has not met. Of course, Abel was no stranger to Cain, but his very brother. Consider, too, that Abel was a shepherd who protected sheep from wolves, while Cain slaughtered Abel as a wolf does a sheep.

The significance of this Latin proverb has been debated throughout the centuries. The seventeenth-century British philosopher Thomas Hobbes would write, for example, that men are like *men* to other men *within their own cities or societies* but are like *wolves* to *outsiders.* The highly influential twentieth-century Viennese psychiatrist Sigmund Freud would declare that human beings are not gentle beings seeking love but are aggressive beings who see others as possible helpers or sexual partners, as well as objects for their aggression in the form of robbery, humiliation, sexual and other forms of abuse, torture, and even murder. Indeed, he concludes his ponderings on the subject in his *Civilization and Its Discontents* with that Latin proverb—*Homini homo lupus!*

Unfortunately, though psychiatry and clinical psychology have, in our time, moved far from Freud in many respects, Freud's theories on human nature have remained far more well known and influential than those of St. Thomas Aquinas. Freud declared that deep within man lies a cauldron of seething passions. Our *ids* would rein over us with rampant passions for lust and violence, if not feebly restrained by our fragile *egos* and the culture-bound restraining niceties of our *superegos.* Deep down, the id is us. Why should I, says Freud, be my brother's keeper? He would just as soon do me harm. Yes, there we go again: *homini homo lupus!*

Six hundred years before Sigmund, Thomas wrote extensively about our passions and animal appetites as well, including the *concupiscible* appetite through which we desire the things that we *love* and bring us pleasure (food and sex most prominently at the physical level), and through the *irascible* appetite, in which our *ire* (anger) can motivate us to battle against things that we *hate,* things that serve as obstacles to our obtaining what we love. We see these appetites clearly in the behaviors of predatory animals, such as wolves. They spend much of their lives seeking out food, mates, and territories (which provide access to food and mates), and most of their aggression against each other involves conflicts over those very things. On these basic facts I think Freudians and Thomists would agree, but Thomas proffers different principles that make all the difference.

For one thing, the human tendency to have difficulty in controlling our more animalistic appetites lies in the fact that we are fallen creatures, due to the lingering effects of Original Sin, courtesy of Cain and Abel's parents, the parents of us all. Further, while Freud wrote of the ego and the superego as relatively weak and ineffective components of our psychology in comparison with the animalistic id, Thomas, echoing Aristotle and other ancient philosophers, including the Stoics, highlighted the fact that humans are the uniquely *rational* animal, and our unique God-given powers of reason can be developed by our own efforts, and perfected with God's grace, to give us significant mastery over our animal impulses.

Further, through our reason and God's revelation, we can discern moral laws and objective standards of moral behavior that transcend the fragile Freudian superego, supposedly composed merely of contemporary moral rules and prohibitions inculcated in us by our parents and society at large when we are young children. Indeed, this capacity to use our reason to find objective truths and moral principles, and to help rein in our animal passions, is the very stuff of the *virtues*. Virtues perfect our rational powers to obtain truth, to regulate our sexual and aggressive behaviors, and to treat others not with lust or aggression, not as potential victims or burdens, but as fellow beings made in the image and likeness of God, worthy of brotherly love. Indeed, to modern psychology's credit, in recent decades a growing appreciation of "cognitive therapies" that focus on the power of reason to regulate emotion, and even therapies that focus on the development of virtues themselves, have indeed moved us away from the Viennese doctor and toward the Angelic Doctor!

So, although we may well still harbor tendencies and temptations to act wolfishly at times, we can never legitimately treat others badly and claim that our ids, let alone the devil, *made* us do it![36] Further, the Angelic Doctor can help us build the kinds of *virtues* that can help us slam shut the lids on our ids and shoo away our wolfish ways, as we will see in detail a few sections down the road.

He Ain't Heavy, He's My Brother

This phrase is the title of an incredibly poignant song from the 1960s, and it has had even more significance to me because of a visit to Omaha, Nebraska, in 2016. It was then and there that I learned a story that occurred about a hundred years before. In 1918, a boy named Harold Loomis had been left by his mother at an orphanage. His young body was ravaged with polio, and he wore heavy leg braces, which made walking difficult and going up and down stairs particularly burdensome. It wasn't long before several other orphan boys started taking turns carrying Harold up and down the stairs on their backs. One day, the director of the orphanage asked one Reuben Granger if carrying Harold was hard. Reuben replied, "He ain't heavy, he's my brother."

Many years later, in 1943, the director saw a photo in a magazine of a boy carrying another boy on his back with the caption, "He ain't heavy, he's my brother." He wrote the magazine,

---

[36] In chapter 12 we will take a look at the role the devil might play in regard to sin.

requesting permission to use the photo and the caption, which went on to achieve worldwide renown as the image and motto of that orphanage. The director was Father Edward J. Flanagan (1886–1948) and that orphanage was, and is known to this day, as Boys Town — though now they provide their residential care to young girls as well.

What a wonderful life lesson is captured in that phrase! Christ told us to take up our crosses and follow Him (Matt. 16:24; Mark 8:34; Luke 9:23; 14:27). At times, we must suffer like Christ — even little children, such as those in Boys Town who could not be raised by their parents. And yet Christ also told us that He would give us rest, for His yoke is easy and His burden is light (Matt. 11:28–30). St. Aelred of Rievaulx (a medieval Cistercian) expanded on this passage as follows:

> Yes, his yoke is easy and his burden light: therefore you will find rest for your souls. This yoke does not oppress, but unites; this burden has wings, not weight. This yoke is charity. This burden is brotherly love.[37]

When the boys of Boys Town put on their "yokes" and took the burden of Harold on their backs, they reported in their own words that he was not heavy at all, in their most touching and graphic display of brotherly love. Harold was uplifted by the love of his spiritual brothers, and certainly each of them was uplifted spiritually as well, by following what Christ said was the second greatest of all the commandments: to love one's neighbor as oneself.

St. Catherine of Siena (1347–1380) has also chimed in on this loving theme. God has given us our neighbors as a means

---

[37] Aelred of Rievaulx, *The Mirror of Charity*, trans. Elizabeth Connor (Kalamazoo, MI: Cistercian Publications, 1990), 133.

to show our love for Him, and this love should be displayed especially to those "close at hand, under your eyes, as to whom, I say, you are all obliged to help one another by word and doctrine, and the example of good works, and in every other respect in which your neighbor may be seen to be in need."[38] So important is this love of neighbor that the Father spelled it for her in a mystical experience in these thought- and love-provoking words:

> I could easily have created men possessed of all that they should need both for body and soul, but I wished that one should have need of the other, and that they should be My ministers to administer the graces and the gifts that they have received from Me.[39]

So then, we are indeed intended to be our brothers' and our sisters' keepers. We are not to be like wolves to one another, or even, strictly speaking, merely like men or women, but we are called to be like God, loving and ministering to one another as He loves and administers grace to each one of us, and loving one another *through* our love of Him, and as a means of expressing our love for Him, who gave life both to us and to our neighbors. But what kinds of sins can keep us from living this beautiful life lesson? To these we now turn.

The Burden of Inordinate Self-Love

St. Thomas notes that, in a general sense, "it is evident that inordinate self-love is the cause of every sin" (I-II, 77, 4). We

---

[38] *The Dialogue of St. Catherine of Siena* (Charlotte, NC: St. Benedict Press, 2006), 12.

[39] Ibid, 16.

sin whenever we choose limited, earthly goods that will bring us pleasure, ease, or some kind of temporal satisfaction even though they are immoral and oppose God's laws. Such choices show that we love our lower selves more than we love God. St. Catherine reports how God expounded on this lesson to her:

> Self-love, which destroys charity and affection and affection towards the neighbor, is the principle and foundation of every evil. All scandals, hatred, cruelty, and every sort of trouble proceed from this perverse root of self-love, which has poisoned the entire world, and weakened the mystical body of the Holy Church, and the universal body of believers in Christian religion; and therefore, I say to you, that charity gives life to all the virtues, because no virtue can be obtained without charity, which is pure love of Me.[40]

St. Catherine lived in the fourteenth century, another troubled time for the world and the Church, with a multitude of sorrows from wars, to plagues, to scandals and schisms rending the Church apart. Undaunted, St. Catherine wrote to bishops and popes and played no small part in restoring some measure of unity. In fact, she is known as the "Doctor of Unity." In many ways, our time is like hers. We need merely look at the daily headlines to find scandal after scandal, within and outside the Church, caused by perverse self-love that seeks to satisfy desires for sexual pleasure and power over others, sometimes through the most heinous of acts. And sadly, as the twentieth century brought forth the splendor of loving charity directed to the orphaned and troubled boys of Boys Town, in the twenty-first century, we

---

[40] Ibid, 14.

have heard numerous stories of boys and young men (and some girls and women too) who have suffered abuse at the hands of those entrusted as God's shepherds, who have acted instead like Satan's wolves.

Precisely because the facts of widespread clerical abuse of children and adults are so disturbing, we must strive more than ever to live this chapter's life lesson to show all the victims Christ's love. We must always be on the alert to share such love with *everyone* we meet, simply because Christ bids us to do so, bearing in mind as well *that those whom we happen to meet, and perhaps even some we know well, may have suffered some form of abuse in their past of which we have no knowledge.* Our call with this lesson is to love our neighbors and to strive to lighten whatever kinds of loads they might carry. We will be far better suited to do this when we work to quash our inordinate self-love, in whatever form it might take.

Removing the Crushing Yoke of the Big Green Monster Inside Us

Years ago, in suggesting a vivid memory image[41] for the deadly sin of envy, I suggested the image of a man with a face as green as that of the big green fictional monster and superhero the Incredible Hulk. The suggestion for this striking, hopefully

---

[41] Thomas told us that, to remember a thing, we "should take some suitable yet unwonted illustration of it, since the unwonted strikes us more, and so makes a greater and stronger impression on the mind.... Now the reason for the necessity of finding these illustrations or images, is that simple and spiritual impressions easily slip from the mind, unless they be tied as it were to some corporeal image, because human knowledge has a greater hold on sensible objects" (II-II, 49, 1).

memorable image simply built upon the common phrase of a person being "green with envy." Envy has been called a "just vice," not because it promotes the virtue of justice that we just examined, but because the unpleasant emotions associated with envy serve as their own automatic, built-in punishment, making the envier feel rather "green at the gills," to use an idiom usually associated with nausea. It is not fun to be envious, and it is not the kind of sin many will admit to, and much less brag about because it is a petty thing, and yet envy is alive and very unwell within so many souls in our world today, perhaps indeed within our own.

With Thomas as our guide, we might think of envy not merely as green, but also just as fittingly as "blue," since envy involves our *sadness* over another person's good. *Envy does not lift our brothers or sisters, but feels sad when others lift them, or when they lift themselves!* Thomas so perceptively notes that as the sin of *sloth* or *acedia* most directly opposes the Great Commandment to love God with all that we are, because it is a sadness or apathy regarding the good of God, *envy* most directly opposes that second Great Commandment, to love our neighbors as ourselves, because it is a sadness regarding the good of our neighbors. We do not feel green or blue, envious or sad, when some good thing comes our way, and neither should we when some good comes to our neighbor, especially some spiritual good that uplifts his soul.

We can see if envy is working in our souls when we observe our reaction when we hear of some good thing that has come to someone we know well, perhaps a sought after job, a promotion, acknowledgment for a special achievement, or a spiritual transformation. Do we "Rejoice with those who rejoice, weep with those who weep," as St. Paul advises (Rom. 12:15)? Or rather, does another's cause for rejoicing produce in us that gnawing sadness of envy? Envy does not necessarily want what that other person has but is sad that the other person has it! (Does not its pettiness ring out loud and clear?)

Thomas notes that we can see envy in operation when we observe the workings of its daughters, such as *tale-bearing* and *malicious gossip*, whereby we try to bring down a notch, in the eyes of others, the person we envy; perhaps in *detraction*, wherein, face-to-face with the person we envy, we tease or joke with her in a way that belittles the good that has come her way, perhaps by diminishing its importance or comparing it with someone else's greater accomplishment. If our efforts and tale-bearing or detraction have hit their mark, have we felt *joy at the other's misfortune*, another of envy's petty daughters? If our envious efforts have been to no avail, has our failure to produce harm left us *grieving at another's prosperity*, feeling sad that we were unable to spoil our neighbor's good? If such a process has gone on within us, do we grasp that these thoughts, feelings, words, and deeds fuel a sinful *hatred*? This final sinful daughter of envy, hatred, is clearly the opposite of the call to and virtue of charity.

If we are to seek to lighten our neighbor's burdens by embracing the light yoke of charity, we must cast off the green hulking yoke of *envy* in *ourselves* and in *our society*. We saw that justice has its interpersonal (commutative) and larger societal (distributive) dimensions. Envy, which opposes justice as well as charity, can also be seen in interpersonal and broader societal forms. Those who would destroy property rights, for example, would rob others of their legitimate, hard-earned material goods. Thomas addresses rights both to personal property and shared common goods in II-II, 66, 1–2. Given today's growing acceptance of socialist ideas, it is worth recalling a statement of Pope Pius XI in his 1931 encyclical *Quadragesimo Anno*: "No one at the same time can be a good Catholic and a true socialist" (120), a statement preceded and echoed to some extent by every pope from Leo XIII through Benedict XVI, and indeed, even outside the Church. Note well the title of prominent German social scientist Helmut Schoeck's classic work on the dangers of egalitarian and totalitarian governments: *Envy: A Theory of Social Behavior*, (Liberty Fund, 1987). We cannot lift up our neighbors or build a better society merely by taking away the material goods and resources of those we envy.

The Lightness and Warmth of the Virtue of Charity

"Neighbor," "brother," "friend": Thomas tells us the exact term matters little to the God-given virtue of charity, as we saw in this chapter's opening quotation. Christ told us to "love our neighbors as ourselves." We should be aware that outside the Christian faith, and in some very prominent religions, believers will also proclaim the call to love their neighbor, but "neighbor" has a very restricted meaning, referring *only* to those of the same religion, and not to outsiders or "infidels." According to Christ's message, though, metaphorically speaking, *everyone* is our neighbor, brother, and friend, meaning literally that our love should extend to *all* persons on earth, even if they do not share our religion. Out of love we will share the Good News of Christ with them through discussion and loving actions, but never at the point of a sword.

In his extensive treatise on charity (II-II, 23-46), Thomas spells out the many-splendored ways love is to reach out far, wide, and warmly to others. St. Thomas compares the love of charity to the heat of a powerful furnace (II-II, 27, 7). When our hearts burn with the fires of charity, their far-reaching flames will serve to warm strangers and even our enemies. But as those closest to the furnace receive the most heat, true charity (like justice) should begin at home and be directed in greatest intensity to the Spirit who dwells in our hearts and to those who are near to us — our families, friends, school- or workmates, neighbors, and fellow parishioners.

Of course, furnaces themselves are also very hot, and Thomas makes clear that we are indeed called to love *ourselves*, and even our *own bodies* with the love of charity, as we'll examine in our next life lesson. But for now, how can we fan the flames of the charity God places in our hearts so they will warm our neighbors' hearts and waft their burdens away up in smoke?

Although charity, as a theological virtue, is infused into our hearts by God and is potentially infinite in quantity, it can increase or decrease in us through our actions. St. Thomas tells us with moving eloquence how each act of charity increases within us the disposition or tendency for more charitable acts, "and this readiness increasing, breaks out into an act of more fervent love, and strives to advance in charity, and then this charity increases actually" (II-II, 24, 6). Once more, Aristotle says that we become builders by building and harpists by playing the harp. So, too, Thomas tells us we become fervent lovers by loving fervently!

One of my favorite Aquinas quotes is this: "The love of our neighbor requires that not only should we be our neighbor's well-wishers, but also his well-doers" (II-II, 32, 5; cf. 1 John 3:18). Charity is a dynamic virtue that acts and works and gets good things done, all by, with, and in our love for God. So then, let us ask ourselves what loving act will *we* do to lift up our neighbor when we next set this book aside? Let's take just a minute to formulate our plan, and then get back to business.

Praying for Our Neighbors, Especially the Heavily Burdened

The Irish have a name for prayers directed only to our own needs — "stingy prayers"! If we are to lift up and to love our neighbors, our prayers to God must keep their needs in mind too. Such prayer is directly opposed both to inordinate self-love and to the vice of envy. When we envy, we are sad for another's good, a sadness we may come to relish as the next best thing to having what the envied person has. To thank God for the goodness He has bestowed on the person envied and to petition Him to keep that good coming is a pretty direct counterattack on envy and every one of its daughters. Indeed, if you pray for the welfare of the people you envy, you are certainly not envying very well!

We can also ask God to help eradicate any remaining envy within our own hearts, and we can pray for those who might envy us. Further, we can pray for God's grace and strength for those who feel most burdened and need it the most, asking that we might be given the grace and strength to act toward them as instruments of His love, sharing with Him in some of the heavy lifting.

Of course, the prayer Christ gave us is anything but a "stingy prayer," as revealed in its first words: "*Our* Father." We acknowledge that God is our Father and we are brothers and sisters in Christ, and then after praising God, all of our petitions are asked for one another, giving *us*, forgiving *us*, and delivering *us*.

The Sweet Yoke of the Sacraments

How can the sacraments strengthen our love of neighbor and give us the strength to lift up our brothers and sisters in Christ? Of course, it is the sacrament of *Baptism* that joins us all together as brothers and sisters in Christ. It bestows on us the sweet yoke of Christ and the graces of the Holy Spirit that make that yoke light. It also allows us to share in the blessings of one another's merits and virtues. Consider these wise words of Venerable Louis of Granada (1505–1588) on pulverizing envy and practicing charity among those who are baptized:

> If you continue in a state of grace, united to your neighbor through charity, you have a share in all his good works, and the more he merits, the richer you become. So far, therefore, from envying his virtue, you should find it a source of consolation. Alas! Because your neighbor is advancing, will you fall back? Ah! If you would love him in the virtues which you do not find in yourself, you would share in them through charity; the profit of his labors would also become yours.[42]

The sacrament of Baptism should remind us that we're all in this together, *this* being that race for the eternal prize of bliss in heaven, and we're all here to help one another to cross God's finishing line.

Indeed, in the sacrament of *Confirmation*, God bestows upon us the extra strength we need to cross that goal. In this sacrament, we become soldiers for Christ, mature and confident members of what has long been called the Church Militant of believers on earth. A classic act of military honor is the soldier's vow to leave no soldiers behind. When ancient Romans proclaimed, *"Nemo resideo!"* they echoed in their own tongue the principle of even more ancient Greek warriors. As warriors for Christ, we should also strive to leave no one behind, to exert our strength to lift

---

[42]   Louis of Granada, *The Sinner's Guide* (New York, NY: Veritatas Splendor Publications, 2012), 289.

those who need uplifting and to do our best to rescue the bodies and souls of our neighbors who have been captured by the harmful, sinful secular ideologies proclaimed and endorsed in our time.

Of course, the ultimate act of neighborly love is to give one's life for a friend (John 15:13), and this Christ did for us. Let us recall how He picked up the burden of the physical Cross, knowing the suffering He would endure upon it, so that we could be uplifted and forgiven of our sins. Let us recall how Simon of Cyrene was compelled to help Christ carry that Cross (Matt. 27:32; Mark 15:21; Luke 23:26), and how Christ told us that what we do for the least of our brothers, we do for Him (Matt. 25:40). Will we heed Christ's example and help our brothers and sisters with their burdens? Will we remember that, like St. Paul, we can do all things in Christ, who strengthens us (Phil. 4:13), and that every time we receive the *Eucharist* we receive that unlimited source of strength Himself in His Body, Blood, Soul, and Divinity?

LIFE LESSON 5 SUMMA

There is no brother or sister so heavy that God cannot give us the strength to strive to help lift him or her up. We were made to be our brothers' and sisters' keepers and to strive to pulverize all manner of sins, especially the petty sin of envy, which makes us saddened by our neighbor's good fortune. Rather, we must fan the flames of our loving charity and try to warm our neighbors with additional spiritual and, when needed, material goods. We must pray every day not only for ourselves, but for all our brothers and sisters in Christ, united as children of God through the sacrament of Baptism and made firm and given the strength we need to lift one another up through the sacrament of Confirmation.

Lesson 6

Be Your Own Best Friend

We cannot fully love others unless we love our highest selves.

Isn't it sinful to love yourself?

Thomas answers that ...

"Just as unity is the principle of union,
the love with which a man loves himself is
the form and the root of friendship."

—*Summa Theologica* II-II, 25, 4

The Natural Form and Root of Friendship

In examining our second life lesson on focusing on what matters the most and our fifth life lesson about the love of our neighbor, we've seen twice before that Thomas told us plainly enough that "inordinate self-love is the cause of every sin" (I-II, 77, 4). "Inordinate" was noted to mean disordered, unrestrained, and inappropriate—the love of the lower, bodily, animal self over one's spiritual soul, love of simple pleasures, of money, of false gods of every sort in place of love for God. Harking back further to the theme of our first life lesson, *sin*, the fruit of inordinate self-love, means *accepting what is infinitely far less than the best.* How then can it be that "the love with which a man loves himself is the *form* and the *root* of friendship?" Good question.

Let's start with *form*. When Thomas speaks of form, he echoes Aristotle regarding two internal causes of anything, the *material* and the *formal* cause. Anything's material cause refers to the matter *out of which* the thing is made, while the formal cause refers to that *which makes a thing into what it is*. For a simple example going back to Aristotle, consider an elaborate wax seal, like the kind that used to personalize and seal letters closed. The wax is the matter, and the engraved stamp has provided the form. There is no personalized wax seal without *both*, and indeed, far higher things than wax seals are also composed of matter and form. The Philosopher elaborated and extrapolated as follows: "We can dismiss the question of whether the soul and body are one; it is as though we were to ask whether the wax and its shape are one."[43]

Take, for example, all the matter that composes a mature human body or even those original two cells from one's mother and one's father from which one's body begins. The physical body is a human's material cause. Human beings need bodies, as does every other life form on earth. Angels do not have bodies, but that's another story we will tell in chapter 10. A dead person's body, however, is not a fully human being, but is referred to as a corpse, from the Latin word *corpus*, "body." The reason it is now merely a body and not a living human being is because it no longer has its *form*, that which transforms the flesh of the body into a human being, an inanimate body into an animate one. And the thing that is the *form* is precisely the *soul*, in Latin the *anima*, that entity with the first function of producing life.

---

[43]   *On the Soul*, bk. 2, chap. 12, cited in Jonathan Barnes, ed., *The Complete Works of Aristotle* (Princeton, NJ: Princeton University Press, 1984), 657.

Indeed, the Church teaches that "the unity of soul and body is so profound that one has to consider the soul to be the 'form' of the body: i.e., it is because of its spiritual soul that the body made of matter becomes a living, human body; spirit and matter, in man, are not two natures united, but rather their union forms a single nature."[44]

So, when Thomas speaks of the love of a man for himself as the "form" of friendship, he means that a person's natural love for his own welfare is something indispensable to the formation of relationships with other people in which they are seen and treated not as enemies but as friends. We'll elaborate aplenty in the pages ahead, but for now let's look at that other key word, "root."

What did St. Thomas consider the "root" of friendship? He told us explicitly: "Just as unity is the principle of union, the love with which a man loves himself is the form and root of friendship" (II-II, 25, 4). *Self-love*, then, is not only the *form* that gives friendship life, but the *root* of friendship as well. But what exactly does Thomas mean by a "root"?

Elsewhere in the *Summa Theologica* (I-II, 84, 1), when expounding upon the meaning of the word "root" in 1 Timothy 6:10: "The desire of money is the root of all evil," Thomas explains that in the same way that the root provides sustenance to the whole tree, money serves as the means to satisfy all kinds of worldly desires for the greedy man. Self-love, then, we might conclude, is that which provides sustenance to the tree of friendship, serving as the solid grounding of friendship and as something absolutely necessary to serve the needs that arise in friendship.

---

[44] CCC 365, citing the Council of Vienne, 1312.

When self-love also makes its striking appearance in the *Summa Theologica* as "the cause of every sin," the key additional word that makes all the difference in the world and beyond it is "inordinate." Thomas expounds in his treatment of the causes of sin that such inordinate self-love produces contempt for God, and while he notes there that "well-ordered self-love, whereby a man desires a fitting good for himself is right and natural," it is in the examination of charity that he shows how ordinate, proper, well-ordered, or fitting self-love is indeed the root of friendship—of friendship with others and friendship with God. It is in this sense that our life lesson prescribes becoming one's own best friend!

It is particularly from Aristotle that Thomas concludes that self-love is the "root" and "form" of friendship, citing *Nicomachean Ethics* 9, that "the origin of friendly relations with others lies in our relations to ourselves." And yet, characteristically for Thomas, even before this elaboration, he has cited a scriptural foundation: "It is written (Lev. 19:18): *Thou shalt love thy friend as thyself.*" Thomas then elaborates upon Aristotle's description of *what appropriate self-love is*, that of *love of our higher nature and the perfection of our reason rather than the inordinate self-love that seeks merely to serve our sensitive, animal wants and needs.* Further, Thomas elaborates that love of self is the model of love for others, and as models are more excellent than their copies, *in that sense* the appropriate kind of love of self is *more excellent* even than the love of neighbor.

When Thomas addresses how sinners do not truly love themselves in II-II, 25, 7, expounding upon Psalm 10:6: "He that loveth iniquity, hateth his own soul" (Douay-Rheims), he draws from Aristotle's insights that the five things proper to friendship are what build upon a man's appropriate self-love:

1. A friend desires his friend to be, to exist.
2. A friend desires good things for his friend.

3. A friend does good deeds for his friend.
4. A friend takes pleasure in his friend's company.
5. A friend is of one mind with his friend, rejoicing and sorrowing in almost the same things.

These are five things that virtuous friends wish for and do for their friends. We can preface them by noting that the noblest, most virtuous friendships have a long history in Western philosophy through the writings of Aristotle and others, as treating a dear friend as "a second self," or "one soul in two breasts." Our love of a "second self" is founded upon our God-given, fully ordinate and natural love of one's "first self," so to speak.

The first element of true friendship can be clearly seen in cases of the loss of a good friend, in the anguish we experience when a good friend no longer exists. When a friend dies, we can feel as if we've lost part of ourselves. Indeed, the love of a dear friend would later form the foundation of the Roman Cicero's entire dialogue on friendship, known as the *Laelius*.

The second element, *goodwill*, is necessary for the development of new friendships. It builds upon the very nature and essence of every person's will — to desire the good for oneself. When we have goodwill for our friends, we wish for them the same kinds of good things we wish for ourselves, and we *rejoice* together when we achieve the good and share in each other's *sorrow* when evil comes our way.

Of course, if we truly wish good things for our friends, we will take action to try to achieve them, just as we act to achieve good for ourselves. *Beneficence*, the third element, the giving of benefits or doing of good deeds for our friends, is truly something fine, noble, and *pleasant*. The giver of benefits, therefore, feels pleased with the person he has been able to benefit (the fourth element of pleasure). The friend has afforded him the opportunity to exercise his beneficence. In that sense, the benefactor has also benefited himself.

Thomas, building on Aristotle, notes that the true, virtuous friend desires the spiritual goods of the "inward man" for his friend, and their wills do not conflict since they desire the same things (the fifth and final element of true friendship deriving from proper self-love).

The wicked, on the contrary, do *not* preserve the integrity of the "inward man" and wish spiritual goods for themselves, they do *not* work toward that end, and they do *not* take pleasure in their own company, because when they examine their hearts, what they find there of the past, present, and future is evil and base. Further, they do not even agree with themselves because of "the gnawings of conscience." The wicked love themselves according to the corruption of the "outward man," but their self-love is not true, but only apparent, since they think themselves good when they're not. Sadly, an unrepentant sinner is not really a friend to others or even to himself. As Thomas sums it up: "The wicked have some share of self-love, in so far as they think themselves good. Yet such love of self is not true but apparent; and even this is not possible in those who are very wicked" (II-II, 25, 7).

If we are to seek out the form and the roots of the appropriate kind of self-love that equips us to love others, the kind of self-love of the higher "inward self" that seeks to raise others higher as well, we must learn to weed out and pulverize the roots of false forms of self-love, one of which we will consider next.

Vainglory and False Self-Love

A very common form of inordinate love of one's lower self that makes us false friends to ourselves, poisons our relations with others, and contaminates our culture at large, is the ages-old vice of *vainglory*. *Inani gloria* (inane or silly glory), in Thomas's words, refers to the desire to be known and praised by others for attributes of our lower selves.

Vainglory is a perversion of the love of charity both for others and for ourselves and may grow within us as a spiritual weed intertwined with the terrible tare that is *envy*. Sometimes we envy the honor and glory that others receive because we are frustrated that we do not have it. The more vainglorious we are, the more likely we are to feel envious when others sing the praises of someone besides us! Still, we are called to strive to do things worthy of praise, to glorify God through our actions, to let our lights shine before men. What, then, is the glory we seek in vain? Vainglorious light says, "Hey, look at me!" while the light of true glory shines "that they see your good works and give glory to your Father who is in heaven" (Matt 5:16).

According to Thomas, there are three ways glory can be vain:

1. The things for which one seeks glory are vain or petty.
2. The persons from whom one seeks glory are uncertain and lacking in judgment.
3. The end for which glory is sought is not to magnify God's honor or to help the spiritual welfare of one's neighbor, but to glorify oneself (II-II, 132, 1).

In a nutshell then, the glory we seek is vain if we seek glory for the *wrong things*, from the *wrong people*, or for the *wrong reasons*.

Thomas, like St. Gregory the Great before him, saw *pride* as the "queen of the vices," the source and font of the seven deadly sins, with *vainglory* as its most closely related offspring. Pride spurns God and glories in one's own excellence, and its spawn of vainglory glories in things far too petty to be truly excellent. We can examine our consciences for vainglory by seeking out its various daughters, from a tendency toward *boasting* about our accomplishments or possessions, to the kind of *obstinacy*, *discord*, and *contentiousness* whereby we try to project our perceived superiority toward others by failing to yield when others make valid points contrary to our own, by refusing to admit we are wrong, or by stubbornly refusing to change our minds even when proven wrong. We can also search our souls for *disobedience*, whereby we fail to obey directives from our bosses or disregard traffic, civil, or canon laws because we believe we always know better.

And speaking of canons, unfortunately, in many ways our modern society seems to have canonized the vice of vainglory in the public arena. Look at many celebrities today who are "famous for being famous," or who become influential public figures for performing inane and sometimes even despicable deeds, especially, in our day, if they do so in some form of "protest," thereby signaling to all their politically correct conception of virtue, while demonizing others and casting them in the worst light. Simply turn on the news any night for all kinds of outlandish antics courtesy of those four death-dealing daughters: *obstinacy*, *discord*, *contentiousness*, and *disobedience*.

Indeed, merely turn on one of your Internet social media platforms to see a fair measure of the same, and indeed, not boatloads, but entire oceans of fleets of that vainglorious daughter *boasting*! In fact, you will need to check *your own* account (and I, alas, *mine*) for the literally "telltale" signs of that last daughter. How much time and energy do we take sharing things that we hope will be "liked"? Does it smack of "inordinate self-love"? Do our posts point too often to the fancy feathers in our caps or to the things of the inward and higher self, the things of the true, the good, and the beautiful?

On Building Great Souls to Love in Ourselves

There is a virtue that directly counters vainglory by disposing us to seek out things truly worth of glory and praise. Aristotle's reason pointed toward it 2,300 years ago, and St. Thomas, aided by revelation, transformed it through Christ about 1,600 years later. Thankfully, this virtue has no expiration date and is waiting for us to start building it in our souls today.

Aristotle noted that we do not criticize the person who strives above all to act justly, through self-control, and in accordance only with virtue. Further, this sort of person rewards himself with the greatest of rewards, because he gratifies his rational intellect, the highest controlling aspect of the soul, through acting voluntarily only for what is noble and excellent. This person most truly loves himself, because this part of the soul truly defines what we are as human beings. *Therefore, the man who truly loves himself will busy himself with praiseworthy actions, not in search of praise, but because of the worthiness of the actions in themselves.* The virtue that equips us to act in ways that are truly worthy of honor and glory was called *megalopsychia* by Aristotle, *magnanimitas* by Thomas, or in plain English, *magnanimity*, literally meaning "greatness of soul."

St. Thomas tells us that "magnanimity by its very name denotes stretching forth of the mind to great things" (II-II, 129, 2). Further, magnanimity is about honor, great honor. Indeed, its subject matter is honor, and its end is great accomplishments. This implies not seeking out displays of honor from others but doing great and honorable acts, whether or not any kind of accolades are forthcoming.

Magnanimity is also closely allied with the virtue of *fortitude*, or courage. How so? Thomas tells us that while fortitude strengthens us in respect to confronting great and difficult evils, magnanimity strengthens us in respect to obtaining great and difficult goods. Fortitude itself becomes strongest when fueled by the vision of great good. The person of true fortitude can endure great hardship because his focus is on great things, such as obeying the will of God, and developing his abilities to their fullest. *The person who appropriately loves his higher "inward," self seeks to stretch forth his soul to the good while helping his neighbor's soul to a good stretch as well.*

The connection of magnanimity with fortitude is also clearly seen in our day, because it takes true courage and greatness to seek out worthy and difficult achievements even when they are not glorious in the eyes of the world, and indeed, when they may be despised. Many who would seek spiritual goods may be ridiculed and scorned by others who seek glory for themselves through things that the world sees as good. Virtually our entire modern advertising and entertainment industries prompt us to try to obtain happiness through material things and through fame for hollow deeds. It is ingrained in our popular, secular culture. Let's ask ourselves how we can work up our ire against the fact that we so often let these cultural trends lead us by the nose. Let's use our noses instead to smell that rat of vainglory, of inordinate self-love, and fortify our spirits to chase it from our souls, as we stretch our hearts and minds toward the things that matter most.

Proper Prayers for Ourselves

While I think my Irish ancestors had a good point about avoiding "stingy prayers" that are all about ourselves, it is, of course, appropriate to pray for our own good too, especially since the greater our souls become, the more generous and loving we can be toward others. Now, to love our *neighbors* as *ourselves*, is of course, the second Great Commandment, according to Jesus, so we are called to pray for *both* and we've noted before how "us" appears in the petitions of the Our Father, and in the Hail Mary as well.

As a prayer to counter the vice of vainglory and the sins that it spawns, a straightforward recommendation is the Glory Be:

> Glory be to the Father, and to the Son, and to the Holy Spirit, as it was in the beginning, is now, and ever shall be, world without end. Amen.

This prayer places glory where it belongs and should remind us that any glory we seek should not be for vain things, but for truly meritorious deeds that will give glory to God and inspire others to do so as well.

Christ's Great Commandments are commandments of charity, which includes love of both self and neighbor. Therefore, another traditional prayer that can help us grow in the charity that disposes us toward appropriate self-love is the Act of Charity:

> O my God, I love Thee above all things, with my whole heart and soul, because Thou art all good and worthy of all love. I love my neighbor as myself for the love of Thee. I forgive all who have injured me and ask pardon of all whom I have injured.

Might we pray this prayer with this chapter's life lesson in mind, so that we might become true friends to ourselves, to become truer friends to our neighbor and to God?

No Greater Love Than This Sacrament

All the sacraments come to us through Christ's loving gift of Himself, but let's briefly highlight three of them that bear quite directly on how a proper love of oneself is the form and root of charitable love of others.

12 Life Lessons from St. Thomas Aquinas

We've seen how virtuous friends treat each other like a "second self," each regarding the friend's welfare as highly as his own. In describing the nature and depth of the profoundest of friendships, even Thomas's pagan philosophical mentor Aristotle would turn time and again to the friendship between a husband and a wife, and between parents and children. Indeed, the man who defined man as not only the "rational animal," but the "political animal," would write that "man is an animal more inclined by nature to connubial than political society" (*ST*, Supplement, 41, 1).[45]

Thomas knew well that families are the earthly models of proper self-love and love of neighbor, and that they are formed and perfected through the heavenly sacrament of *Matrimony*. Through Matrimony each spouse not only acquires a "second self," but the two become as "one flesh" (Gen 2:24; Mark 10:8; Matt.19:5; Eph. 5:31) in the deepest, most intimate bonds of friendship. Have those of us who are married thought about how fostering the proper love of what is highest in ourselves will overflow into love of our spouses? Have we reflected on the ways in which generous acts of love from our spouses have stretched our own souls toward higher things? Of course, God has willed that marital love can also produce new generations of "other selves" we can love — our children in some sense literally being our "second selves" (and third, fourth, fifth, or so on, according to how many God has blessed us with).

As for the ultimate model and example of natural love, old Aristotle has argued that it is seen in the love of a mother for her child. We see this in the natural protectiveness of mothers

---

[45] Citing Aristotle's *Nicomachean Ethics*, 8, 12, "connubial" referring to the married state.

124

in many animal species. Some human mothers have been willing, under dire circumstances, to give away a child to be raised by another, content to know that the child is living and thriving, even if they are never to see the child and receive his love in return. Indeed, we see this in Scripture as well, when a true mother was willing to give her baby away to a false claimant rather than have the child split in two (1 Kings 3:16–38). Wise Solomon knew well the nature of true motherly love based on the love of one's higher, inward self, the capstone of which is God's charity, which protects and nurtures the innocent. Of course, Blessed Mary, Mother of God and Mother of the Church, is the foremost human exemplar of the power of motherly love.

Those who are called to the sacrament of *Holy Orders* are certainly called as well to an appropriate love of the very highest parts of the self, whereby, through God's grace they strive to conform themselves to Christ, to act in His person in the Sacrifice of the Mass, and are empowered to administer the sacraments to others. In accepting Holy Orders, the priest forgoes the physical goods of sexual intimacy with a spouse in order to embrace more fully the spiritual goods of God. It is especially grave and heinous when priests embrace their sinful sexual passions and abuse in any way another person, and even if in the context of relations with a "consenting adult," such acts may be legal, but never moral. Let us pray that those in Holy Orders will live out holy lives and that their ecclesiastical superiors will never actively shield or turn a blind eye toward them and their victims. Let us pray as well for the untold number of priests, who, though sinners like us all, truly strive to honor their vows, to seek and to promote holiness in others by loving the highest parts of themselves, the intellect through which they seek to know God, and the will through which they seek to make their wills in perfect conformity to His.

It is the ultimate sacrament of the *Eucharist*, of course, that teaches us to love the highest part of ourselves above even life itself. "God is love" (1 John 4:8), and His love for us was manifested most fully when He sent His Son to become one of us and to die for us. Thomas tells us that "out of the love of charity with which we love God, we ought to love our bodies" (II-II, 25, 6), and yet he agrees with St. Augustine that "we ought to love our neighbor more than our own body" (II-II, 26, 5). He knew, too, what John made clear: "Greater love has no man than this, that a man lay his life down for his friends" (John 15:13). Jesus displayed perfect self-love in His human and divine natures, never sullying his "inward man" with sin. While He was on earth, His love reached out to His friends, to His disciples, including the beloved disciple, John, to the repentant sinner Mary Magdalene, and to so many others. He also came that we all might be no longer servants but friends (John 15:15).

Of course, Christ is God Himself, but through Christ's loving action and the grace of the Holy Spirit, if *we* love one another and testify that the Father sent the Son to be the Savior of the world, "God abides in us and his love is perfected in us" (1 John 4:12).

The highest form of self-love, then, is to love how God abides within us through the indwelling of the Holy Spirit and through the Real Presence of Christ in the Eucharist. We should express the highest of gratitude that Christ gave us the awesome sacrament through which we who eat His flesh and drink His blood take Him—Body, Blood, Soul, and Divinity—into our own bodies through the *Holy Eucharist*. In the Traditional Latin Mass, after Communion the priest prays that Christ's Body and Blood that he has received will *adhaeret visceribus meis* ("cleave to my innermost parts"). If we are to become "our own best friends," we must never forget that we will never love ourselves more fully than when we love Him who so willingly cleaves to the innermost parts of our bodies and our souls.

LIFE LESSON 6 SUMMA

Since we are to love our neighbors *as ourselves*, we must love what is highest and noblest in ourselves in an appropriate way. It is this appropriate self-love of the rational and spiritual potentials of the "inward" man or woman that grounds our abilities to reach out and love others. We must search our souls and weed out the vice of vainglory and seek to glorify God and enrich others through magnanimous thoughts and acts truly worthy of praise. Let our prayers glorify God, and our actions, in whatever our state of life, do so as well. May those who are married truly come to love their spouses and children as other selves. May those in Holy Orders love what is highest within themselves, so that they can best share the graces of the sacraments with others. May we all recall that Christ gave His sinless self so that we might become His friends, and that the highest forms of self-love are to love how God dwells within us through the indwelling of the Holy Spirit and how Christ Himself cleaves to our innermost parts in the Holy Eucharist. This is how we become our own best friends in the way God intended.

Hate the Sin,
Love the Sinner

*Charity demands that we hate
the sin while loving the sinner.*

Hate the sin, love the sinner? (Who are we to judge?)

*"To correct the wrongdoer is a spiritual almsdeed.
But almsdeeds are works of charity. . . . Therefore,
fraternal correction is an act of charity. . . . The
correction of the wrongdoer is a remedy which
should be employed against a man's sin."*

—*Summa Theologica* II-II, 33, 1

Natural Law, the Law of Concupiscence, and the Changing Laws of the Land

This chapter's Thomistic life lesson is, unfortunately, among the most desperately needed lessons in our time. While sin has been with us since Adam and Eve's Fall, so have institutions of family, church, and state, all around the civilized world, striven to help prevent, contain, or overcome sin. You'll recall from our life lesson two, that Satan's law of concupiscence did not totally eradicate the God-given law of nature. St. Paul wrote telling Romans that in Jews, Greeks, and all the Gentiles on earth, there is a natural moral law "written on their hearts, while their conscience also bears witness" (Rom. 2:15). It is up to us whether we read that writing on our cardiac walls, so to speak, and "do by nature what the law requires" (Rom. 2:14).

Indeed, around the same time St. Paul was writing, a noble pagan Stoic philosopher by the name of Musonius Rufus (ca. A.D. 20–101) was providing the proof of this inborn natural law by the witness he bore. Rufus gleaned lessons from reason and natural law and applied them to some of the very most heated, controversial, and divisive issues in his day, issues that obviously remain so twenty centuries later. Rufus's conclusions are so amazingly consonant with some of the Catholic Church's most profound teachings on the value of human life, family, and society that I consider him a "profound, pagan, pro-family, pro-life philosopher." Summarized below are some of Rufus's most fundamental and striking statements on human sexuality, marriage, procreation, abortion, contraception, and large families, complete with comparative references to paragraphs in the *Catechism of the Catholic Church*.[46]

- Only sexual acts carried out within the bounds of marriage and open to the procreation of life are morally right (lecture 12; cf. CCC 2360–2366, 2390–2391).
- Among the most serious illegitimate sexual practices are adultery and homosexual acts. Both arise from lack of self-control, and homosexual acts are intrinsically

---

[46] For English translations of Rufus's lectures, see Cora Lutz, *Musonius Rufus Fragments* (New Delhi, India: Isha Books, 2013) or Cynthia King, *Musonius Rufus: Lectures and Sayings* (published by William B. Irvine, CreateSpace.com, 2011). These bullet-points first appeared in my book *The Porch and the Cross: Ancient Stoic Wisdom for Modern Christian Living* (Kettering, OH: Angelico Press, 2016).

opposed to nature (lecture 12; cf. CCC 2380–2381, 2357–2359).[47]

- The chief purpose of marriage is that a man and wife will live together and have children (lecture 13; cf. CCC 2366–2367). In Rufus's words: "The primary end of marriage is community of life with a view to the procreation of children."
- Marriage is founded upon mutual love and care "in sickness and in health" (lecture 13; cf. CCC 2360–2361—and in Catholic wedding vows).
- The marriage bond of partnership and union is admirable and beautiful (lecture 13; cf. CCC 2362).
- Anyone who works to destroy marriage destroys family, city, and the human race (lecture 14; cf. CCC 2209–2211).
- Lawgivers were wise to prohibit abortion and methods of artificial contraception (lecture 15; cf. CCC 2366–2367, 2370–2372, 2270–2275).
- Large families are great gifts from God (lecture 15; cf. CCC 2373).

How interesting that such moral truths can be gleaned from the light of the natural law alone! Watch the news in our time and such ideas are almost unfailingly associated with the strictly

---

[47] In the *Summa Theologica*, St. Thomas addresses adultery with the same conclusions based on natural law and Christ's law of love when he explains the parts of the vice of lust in II-II, 154, 8, and when he discusses the sacrament of Matrimony in the Supplement after Part III. He addresses homosexual acts, which CCC 2357 describes as "intrinsically disordered" and Thomas described as *"vitium contra naturam"* (vice contrary to nature) and *"sodomiticum vitium"* (the vice of sodomy) in II-II, 154, 11, citing Romans 1:27.

religious ideas of "the Christian alt-right," with the declaration, or at least the implication, that Christians are seeking to impose their religious views on all the citizenry.

Similar moral truths are found in the writings of many other ancient Greek and Roman philosophers as well. Aristotle, for example, wrote that the morality of many behaviors, such as the expression of anger (as we considered in chapter 3), is determined by whether they are performed with the right people, at the right time, in the right way, and for the right reasons. Other behaviors, however, are intrinsically disordered, *morally wrong by nature*, and there is no right way to express them. He included adultery, for example, as such a violation of natural law. There is simply no right way to do it! The Stoic Epictetus, Rufus's former pupil, spoke out at length about adultery as well, noting how it disgraces and abases the adulterer and harms not only the spouse and the family, but society as a whole.

As we saw in chapter 2, the divine laws revealed to Moses, such as those summarized in the Ten Commandments (Exod. 20:2–7; Deut. 5:6–21; CCC 2051–2052) confirm the natural law and shed even further light upon our moral obligations to each other—and to God. Christ's law of love did not abolish those commandments but condensed and fulfilled its expression in the Great Commandments to love God with all we are and our neighbors as ourselves (Matt. 22:36–40; Mark 12:28–34; Luke 10:25–28).

A few centuries after the time of Musonius Rufus, the Roman emperor Julian the Apostate (330–363), a descendant of the Christian emperor Constantine the Great (272–337), when he renounced his Christianity (albeit an Arian corruption) and strove to restore the ancient pagan religions, would admit that the fourth through tenth commandments, relating to how we deal with one another, are indeed universal and natural moral laws. Further, much to his discomfort, he felt he had no choice but to urge the would-be restorers of pagan religion to imitate the "Galileans," as he slightingly called Christians, in their works of charity, including the establishment of hospitals.

But look at how far we descended in the last two thousand years, *and indeed, in the last few decades, and even the last handful of years*. As I wrote about deadly sins in 2015, I discussed the fact that many sinful behaviors that governments had historically prohibited for the public good were becoming legalized in America and throughout the world. One such hot topic was the push for same-sex "marriage" throughout the nation.[48] The legalized killing of the unborn had, of course, been the law of the land in the United States since 1973. Since I wrote just a few years ago, same-sex "marriage" has become the law of the land, and not only in the United States. Ireland, for example, legalized same-sex "marriage" late in 2015, and the same "land of saints and scholars" legalized abortion in 2018.

What has changed, or become more pronounced, *even in the last few years*, however, is not merely the *legalization* of immoral

---

[48] And here is one reason I used the quotation marks. Such "marriages" can never be consummated, consummation referring to the intercourse of the male husband and female wife in the marital and potentially reproductive act. No amount of politically correct thinking or "identifying" as married can contravene nature and the natural laws of sexual reproduction. Some may argue there are more than two sexes and point to some rare genetic variants in which people are born with extra sexual chromosomes and ambiguous or extra sexual organs, such as is found in rare cases of hermaphroditism, but this does not alter the fact that two individuals of the same sex are unable to reproduce with each other, in accordance with the laws of nature.

acts by governmental bodies, but their active *promotion* and *attempts to normalize*, and even *glamorize*, acts that violate natural laws.[49] Further, people are increasingly forced to pay for and subsidize acts they recognize as morally reprehensible, such as abortion. People who proclaimed decades back, "If you don't like abortion, don't get one!" have changed their belief, if not the words of their slogan, to "If you don't like abortion, too bad, pay for mine!"[50]

Further, people in the United States and other Western nations are becoming increasingly pressured to speak and act against

[49] For example, in November 2018, Pope Francis would note "in our societies it even seems that homosexuality is fashionable." "In New Book on Clergy and Religious Life, Pope Francis Addresses Homosexuality," Catholic News Agency, November 30, 2018, https://www.catholicnewsagency.com/news/in-new-book-on-clergy-and-religious-life-pope-francis-addresses-homosexuality-27409.

[50] Indeed, even since the few weeks past when I first wrote these words, state legislators and governors in New York, Virginia, and in other states, have passed or promoted laws amounting not only to abortion of the unborn, but to infanticide of children who survive failed abortions. In New York, this law was celebrated with smiles, cheers, and the lighting up in pink of the One World Trade Center (perhaps overlooking the fact that roughly half of aborted babies are female). Alas, the house and senate of my own state of Illinois have passed an even more heinous bill. See, for example, Catholic News Agency, "Illinois Bishops Denounce Rush to Advance 'Reproductive Health Act,'" *National Catholic Register*, May 29, 2019, http://www.ncregister.com/daily-news/illinois-bishops-denounce-rush-to-advance-reproductive-health-act; or "Update: Illinois House Oks Abortion Bill; Vote Called 'Collective Moral Failing,'" Catholic News Service, May 30, 2019, https://www.catholicnews.com/services/englishnews/2019/illinois-house-oks-abortion-bill-vote-called-collective-moral-failing.cfm.

their consciences, as opponents of natural law seek to have their cake and eat it too, sometimes literally, whether forcing bakers to bake cakes in endorsement of same-sex "marriages" or forcing teachers to call a student with XY chromosomes (a male) "she," and a person with XX chromosomes (a female) "he." Such trends threaten freedom *of* religion and *freedom* of speech to replace them with freedom *from* religion and *forced* speech.

Even within the Church, we are scandalized by cases of sexual abuse of children, of teens, and of young seminarians and priests by older priests and prelates, approximately 80 percent of which have been found by studies, time and again, to involve the predation of post-pubescent adolescent *males*.[51] Simply to point this fact out is routinely met by some priests and bishops with knee-jerk responses, implying that one is suggesting that *all* homosexuals are sexual abusers, which is clearly *not* the case. Some abusers are indeed heterosexuals, but they are far less likely to be credibly accused of abuse within the Catholic Church.

We find within the Church, as well, strong pressures to *identify* individuals by their sexual preferences. The acronym "LGBT," for instance (why not spell it out as Lesbian, Gay, Bisexual, and

---

[51] According to page 12 of the USCCB-commissioned 2004 John Jay report, 81 percent of clerical abuse victims were male. Astoundingly, some people have argued that this does not implicate homosexuality as an offender risk factor, confounding the abuse with a *generalized pedophilia* that seeks out whatever child victims are available. The vast majority of abuse victims were not pre-pubescent children, and their abuse can be more specifically classified as acts of *ephebophilia* from the Greek *ephebos* for "adolescents." A full 78 percent of the victims from 1950 to 2002 were adolescents ages eleven to seventeen. Note that the World Health Organization defines adolescents as persons between the ages of ten and twenty-four.

Transsexual?) has appeared, for the first time in 2018, in a pre-synodal working document of the Catholic Church, *Instrumentum Laboris*, referencing "LGBT youth" in paragraph 197. It did not appear in the synod's final document, but we must note that some in the Church would indeed prefer that we identify a person's *essence* as a human being and child of God by his or her sexual inclinations. This could hardly be further from a Thomistic understanding of foundational *essences* and nonessential *accidents* of the human being.

Further, some prelates within the Church would have us legitimize the concept of "transgenderism," implying that when "male and female he created them" (Gen. 5:2) God Himself was woefully unenlightened with such limited "binary thinking" regarding the human sexes, not to mention completely unaware of the modern world's plethora of "genders."[52]

Well, what are we to do today, if we believe in the facts of nature and of natural law, not to mention the law of Moses and the law of Christ? Must we remain silent, or must we speak out? How are we to act toward people we know, perhaps some of those most dear and close to us who have either embraced or actively promote a variety of fashionable sinful behaviors? What if *we* have done so or continue to do so? Who are we to judge, after all? These questions are so controversial and perplexing that it's time we turned to Thomas.

[52] One social media giant offered a mere fifty-eight gender choices in 2014 but was up to seventy-one at the time of this writing. I will not weigh readers down with any direct references to articles. A simple Internet search on "number of genders in humans" yielded 9,420,000 results in 0.73 seconds on the morning of February 18, 2019.

How Hate Should Act Only in the Service of Love

I tried to lay down the natural law in our first section to show that we really are capable of judging what kinds of behaviors are sinful, even if we merely adhere to the natural law accessible to all through human reason. Still, according to Christ's law of love, we are admonished *not* to judge *persons* — "Judge not, that you be not judged" (Matt. 7:1) — but we are indeed called to judge sinful *behaviors* and certainly *not* to *promote* them. Again, in Christ's words: "Whoever causes one of these little ones who believe in me to sin, it would be better for him to have a millstone fastened around his neck and to be drowned in the depths of the sea" (Matt. 18:6). Christ will judge us all at the Last Judgment. He will have the final word of judgment on every person's soul, but He does call on *us* to judge sinful behaviors in *ourselves*, and also in *others*, if we desire for ourselves and for our neighbors a Last Judgment that awards us eternal bliss in heaven.

Here, then, we have the gist of the extremely important and legitimate lesson to "hate the sin, but love the sinner." I've heard some people dismiss this concept as some sort of a disingenuous posture or even an absurd statement. How can we possibly hate what a person does while we love that person? To argue about the immoral nature of homosexual acts, of surgical destruction of one's sexual organs, or of slaughtering babies in the womb is to face charges that one *hates people* with same-sex attraction, gender dysphoria,[53] or those who've had abortions or support abortion for others. This is surely faulty logic.

---

[53] This is the current term for the officially classified psychiatric disorder in the *Diagnostic and Statistical Manual of the American Psychiatric Association*, 5th ed. (DSM-5), replacing the older term "gender identity disorder." It "involves a conflict between a

12 Life Lessons from St. Thomas Aquinas

Imagine the case of a loved one, perhaps a close family member, who is addicted to heroin, cocaine, crystal meth, or some other drug that has broken apart relationships, damaged his physical and mental health, and perhaps left him jobless, homeless, or incarcerated. (Sadly, many, if not most readers can probably think of such a person in their lives.) Now, does it not make the greatest sense to *hate* the drug-abusing *behavior* precisely *because* we *love* the *person* who has become addicted, as well as others who suffer collateral damage because of the addiction, perhaps their children, for one especially salient example?

Let's call in Thomas now for some important explication to see how hatred and love are related. "Hatred of the evil that is contrary to one's natural good is the first of the soul's passions, even as love of one's natural good is" (II-II, 34, 6). By our natures we love what we believe to be good. *Love* moves our wills to seek out the good, and a proper *hatred* comes into play when we will to avoid or remove the bad, harmful, evil things that keep us from the good. In this sense, an appropriate hatred for what is evil *serves* the love of the good.

Thomas makes clear that our *love* of neighbor can and sometimes must be manifested through the *hate of the sin in* our neighbor, *but never through hate of the neighbor himself.* He has posed the formal question "Whether Hated of One's Neighbor Is Always a Sin." To make a long story short, his answer is *yes*, but let him flesh it out:

Now love is due to our neighbor in respect of what he holds from God, i.e., in respect of nature and grace. But

---

person's physical or assigned gender and the gender with which he/she/they identify." (Note that the APA itself is not content with the choices "he" or "she" but introduces for the singular noun "person" the plural pronoun "they.")

140

not in respect of what he has of himself and from the devil, i.e., in respect of sin and lack of justice. Consequently, it is lawful to hate the sin in one's brother, and whatever pertains to the defect of Divine Justice, but we cannot hate our brother's nature and grace without sin. Now it is part of our love for our brother that we hate the fault and the lack of good in him, since desire for another's good is equivalent to hatred of evil. (II-II, 34, 3)

Thomas notes that God Himself, who *is* love, holds to this crucial distinction: "God hates the sin which is in the detractor, not his nature" (ibid.).

Correct Your Brother — and Prepare to Be Corrected

How is such *hatred* of a brother's or sister's *sin*, or anyone's for that matter, to be manifested in such a way that it shows *love* for that *person*? The Church has long taught us of seven *corporal* works of mercy through which we tend to the bodily, physical needs of our neighbors, listed in Thomas's day as "feeding the hungry, giving drink to the thirsty, clothing the naked, harboring the harborless,[54] visiting the sick, ransoming the captive,[55] and burying the dead" (II-II, 32, 2). The Church has also taught seven *spiritual* acts of mercy through which we tend to our neighbor's spiritual needs, listed by Thomas as "to instruct the ignorant, to counsel the doubtful, to comfort the sorrowful, to reprove the sinner, to forgive injuries, to bear with those who trouble and annoy us, and to pray for all" (ibid.).[56]

---

[54] CCC 2447 calls this "sheltering the homeless."
[55] "Visiting the imprisoned" in CCC 2447.
[56] These are summarized as "instructing, advising, consoling, and comforting" in CCC 2247.

In Thomas's language, all fourteen of these almsdeeds[57] are "works of charity through the medium of mercy" (II-II, 32, 1). "Charity" is another word for "love," so each of these fourteen works of mercy is indeed an expression of Christian love. The "almsdeed" or "spiritual work of mercy" at front and center in this chapter's lesson is, of course, "to reprove the sinner." Thankfully, Thomas wrote an entire question with eight articles (II-II, 33) on the subject under the terminology of *correctione fraterna* (fraternal correction).

In the first article, Thomas makes clear that correcting a wrongdoer is "a spiritual almsdeed," an "an act of charity," and "a remedy against a [person's] sin." He makes an extremely important distinction too, noting that a sin may be harmful to the sinner, but it may secondarily be harmful to others too, "by hurting or scandalizing them, or by being detrimental to the public good." Strictly speaking, the aim of fraternal correction is to do away with the sinner's evil and to help him procure the good, which is a direct act of *charity, or love*. When fraternal correction prevents the sinner from harming other individual persons, or even the common good, then it is also an act of *justice*. So, indeed, when we take action to hate a sin, but love a sinner, our hate of sin may serve not only *love*, but the *justice* that gives each person his or her rightful due.

Thomas notes in his second article that fraternal correction is also a "precept," something God bids us to do when we are confronted with someone's sinful behavior, but Thomas clearly advises *against* going about hunting for others' sins to correct,

---

[57] Thomas used the term *eleemosyna*, a Latinization based on the Greek word referring both to showing mercy and to giving alms. In the *Summa Theologica*, it is translated as "almsdeeds."

becoming "spies on the lives of others." Further, when hating the sin and loving the sinner, we must never forget that we ourselves, as sinners, must remain open to fraternal correction ourselves when we merit it. We must also be especially careful never to criticize others for sins that we ourselves excel in! Thomas explicates this principle in his fifth article on fraternal correction. Christ told us not to point out the speck in our brother's eye when a log is stuck in our own (Matt. 7:2–4)! St. Paul expands on the warning of the judgment we will receive from God if we judge another person's sinful actions when we commit the same sins (Rom. 2:1–3).

Now, since "if we say we have no sin, we deceive ourselves" (1 John 1:8), this might seem to put the kibosh on any kind of fraternal correction. Indeed, who are we to judge? Well, both Christ and St. Paul immediately supply the solution to this dilemma. Paul tells us we must first repent of our own sins (Rom. 2:4), and Christ minces no words, telling us: "You hypocrite, first take the log out of your own eye, and then you will see clearly to take the speck out of your brother's eye" (Matt. 7:5). Self-correction must precede fraternal correction in such cases. Not only must we hate our neighbor's sin and love our neighbor; *we must also hate our own sin, while loving ourselves.*

Fraternal correction is clearly no easy thing. Thomas brings up yet another important caveat in his sixth article:

On the contrary. It is written (Prov. 4:8): *Rebuke not a scorner lest he hate thee,* where a gloss remarks: *You must not fear lest the scorner insult you when you rebuke him; rather should you bear in mind that by making him hate you, you may make him worse.* Therefore, one ought to forgo fraternal correction, when we fear lest we may make a man worse.

Surely you can relate to this if you have come across people (such as the contentious "aginners" we mentioned in chapter 3), whom, if you attempt to correct them regarding some behavior (such as being so darn disagreeable!), they will be even more likely to ratchet up their sinful behavior just to spite you. Such folk were around in Thomas's day, and they likely will be in the day of our grandchildren's grandchildren. Hence, we must always try to exercise judgment in whether to correct a particular person at a particular time. Though we should never endorse or reward a person's sinful behavior, we must be prudent to recognize situations where charity and justice bid us *not* to attempt to correct our neighbor, lest we make him worse.

Thomas discusses yet finer, but absolutely essential aspects of fraternal correction in his seventh article, and this regards whether we should correct someone's sinful behavior one on one or publicly. Here, his fundamental insights are provided directly by the Son of God, beginning with these words: "If your brother sins against you, go and tell him his fault, between you and him alone" (Matt. 18:15). Thomas cites St. Augustine, who noted that private corrections aim at a person's amendment while avoiding the kind of public disgrace that might make a person defend his sinful behavior, making him worse, as we just discussed above. He then makes an important distinction: that private, "secret" sins in which a person sins only against you or harms only himself, should ideally be handled privately, at least at first.[58]

---

[58] Christ would go on to clarify that if a brother who sinned against you does not listen to private correction, you should bring along a few others and, if still unsuccessful, take it to the Church or ultimately to the public authorities (Matt. 18:16–17).

When secret sins are harmful to others—for example, when a person plots to betray his country, or when a heretic secretly works to turn people away from the Faith—then it is appropriate to correct such a person publicly, unless one firmly believes that private correction will induce him to stop. "Since, however, one's conscience should be preferred to a good name, Our Lord wished that we should publicly denounce our brother and so deliver his conscience from sin, even though he should forfeit his good name. Therefore, it is evident that the precept requires a secret admonition to precede public denunciation."

A Simple Summary on Pulverizing Sin

Because of the complexities of the issues involved in hating sin out of the love for sinners, we have included not *one*, but *three* sections on "penetrating the principle" of our lesson, the first concentrating on natural law, the second on the appropriate passion of hate, and the third on fraternal correction. Since the focus of this chapter's whole lesson is on sin itself (and hating it), I will curtail this section on "pulverizing sin" to keep our lesson of digestible length.

Please note that, although our focus thus far in this chapter has been on sins that flow from the deadly sin of *lust*, such as the desire for recognition and approval of unnatural sexual behaviors, for behaviors that violate the insolubility of marriage, for sexually abusive behavior toward children or adults, both inside and outside the Church, or even the killing of innocent lives in abortion, our principles apply to all manner of sins. Because of the prevalence of such sexual sins in our modern world, when I have given public talks on the seven deadly sins and have asked for a show of hands for the sins wreaking the most havoc in our world today, lust is the hands-up winner every time. Hence, it has received the most attention here.

Still, we have a responsibility to hate *all manifestations of sin* in others, *and in ourselves*, so we might free others and ourselves from evils that destroy the good in our lives, and indeed, in their extremes, the very lives of the unborn. If we are to fight against sin, we must start that fight within our own souls, difficult as that may be in our culture so saturated with libertinism and unbridled hedonism.

Further, if a person we know openly engages in a sinful life-style or endorses other immoral practices, we must not directly endorse the practices, and we ourselves must not identify the person with his or her actions or lifestyle. He or she, as a person of inherent dignity made in the image and likeness of God, is far more than his or her sexual preferences or behaviors. Further, we should engage such people with warmth, kindness, and love, acknowledging their dignity as persons, and be as quick to lend them a hand to lighten their loads as we would for any other brother, sister, or neighbor, loving them as we love ourselves, through our love of God.

Virtues That Hate Sin and Love Sinners

Which kinds of virtues can help us hate sin but love sinners? First and foremost is the "mother of the virtues," the love that is *charity*. This love of God and love of neighbor and self through Him, should motivate all our actions whenever we confront sin, since we must do so to help and not to hurt others.

For battling the kinds of sexual sins that make up the hotbed issues of our day, I believe that the practice of the *intellectual virtue* of *science* (or *knowledge*),[59] is of paramount importance,

---

[59] The English words "science" and "knowledge" are both used for this virtue called *scientia* by St. Thomas, because the base

because so much misinformation is circulated today in defense of sinful behaviors, including abortion, homosexual activity, and hormonal therapies or surgical operations on individuals, even young children, distressed by their male or female sex. These are all complicated issues, and part of the problem is that they are often presented precisely as if they were *not* complicated. Well, *science* is the intellectual virtue that seeks truth by carefully examining causes and effects, so let's apply the virtue of science to dig into one extremely controversial issue to seek out its true causes and effects.

For example, a well-known priest has recently stated that virtually every competent psychiatrist or biologist acknowledges that people do not choose their sexual orientation any more than they choose to be left-handed. Such statements may suggest the false dichotomy that people either *choose* their sexual orientation or they were "made that way," with the theological implication that *God* made them that way and the biological implication that it is in their *genes*.

So, what is the official position of current psychiatric and psychological experts on the cause of homosexual orientation?

According to a December 2013 position statement of the American Psychiatric Association, "the causes of sexual orientation (whether homosexual or heterosexual) are not known at this time and likely are multifactorial including biological

---

word of "science" means "to know." I prefer to use the term "science," because the modern conception of science tends to be respected in our world today. The ancient meaning, however, is much fuller and more comprehensive, since virtually any topic can be explored through a proper science. Thomas referred to theology, as "sacred science."

and behavioral roots which may vary between individuals and may even vary over time."[60]

The American Psychological Association reports on their current website as follows: "There is no consensus among scientists about the exact reasons that an individual develops a heterosexual, bisexual, gay or lesbian orientation. Although much research has examined the possible genetic, hormonal, developmental, social and cultural influences on sexual orientation, no findings have emerged that permit scientists to conclude that sexual orientation is determined by any particular factor or factors. Many think that nature and nurture both play complex roles; most people experience little or no sense of choice about their sexual orientation."[61]

Most people who make blanket statements about the biological determination of sexual attraction are probably unaware that there is a complete scientific discipline called "behavior genetics" that strives to ferret out the genetic and nongenetic influences on all kinds of human behaviors, characteristics, and diseases. Further, behavioral geneticists have some fairly powerful tools, including the comparison of traits shared by identical, or monozygotic (MZ), twins, who share 100 percent of their genes, and fraternal, or dyzygotic twins (DZ), who share 50 percent of their genes, as do other full brothers and sisters.

Findings from such research are very rarely seen in public discussions of the issue of same-sex attraction. (Have *you* ever seen them reported?)

[60] A PDF of the APA Position Statement on Issues Related to Homosexuality, December 2013, is available online.
[61] American Psychological Association, "Sexual Orientation and Homosexuality," https://www.apa.org/topics/lgbt/orientation. aspx.

Today, researchers can also directly examine people's DNA sequences to explore possible connections between genetic markers and human behaviors. In fall 2018, headlines were made when a large study reportedly showed connections between DNA variants and same-sex behaviors, but the current researchers themselves noted that "there is no gay gene." "We know almost nothing about the genetics of sexual behavior," they said, "so anywhere is a good place to start." They made clear that the four genetic variants found in this study could *not* reliably predict someone's sexual orientation. The correlation was simply far too weak. "There's really no predictive power."[62] In other words, if you knew a person's DNA profile at these four sections, you would not do significantly better than chance at trying to predict whether the person had engaged in same-sex behavior.

I have belabored such points with scientific findings because there is so much propaganda out there today, both outside and inside the Church, that argues that sexual behaviors outside the natural law are not sinful *because they are not voluntary*. Recall that serious sin requires grave matter, full knowledge, and *deliberate consent*. The propagandists argue that *deliberate consent* does not come into play in cases of homosexual behaviors because people do not choose to have a homosexual orientation. This is a potentially highly dangerous slippery slope, especially since the same arguments can be applied to pedophilia, an issue that plagues not only the modern world, but the modern Church.

---

62 Michael Price, "Giant Study Links DNA Variants to Same-Sex Behavior," *Science*, October 20, 2018, https://www.sciencemag. org/news/2018/10/giant-study-links-dna-variants-same-sex-behavior.

Some people already argue that adult-minor sexual acts should not be illegal if the child or adolescent grants assent.[63]

There may well be some kind of limited biologically based *predispositions* that play some role in sexual *orientation* or *attraction* itself, but the *performance* of sexual *acts* with other people does involve consent and choices of our free will. This applies to heterosexual behavior just as it does to homosexual behavior.

The bottom line is that we need to be informed about the realities behind sexual orientation and behavior, from the perspective of natural law, the teachings of the Church, and the scientific findings. We need to hate sins to protect sinners, whom we love, from the soul-wrecking, and sometimes body-wrecking effects of sin and disordered thinking. The last thing we need to do is to turn off our intellects about such matters, to fail to develop the virtue of science within our souls, and unthinkingly pass on the propaganda of the day, doing more harm than good.[64] We must grow in the virtues of science if we are truly to love and help our neighbor.

---

[63]   Indeed, such a person ran for a U.S. Congressional seat in 2018. A quick Internet search of "pedophilia congressman" will provide all the sad details for those who would care for them.

[64]   For a concrete example of medical treatments that may do more harm than good, in my teens I became aware of the psychotherapeutic system of "Psycho-cybernetics" developed by Maxwell Maltz, M.D., in 1960. It was based largely on the power of visualization, self-affirmations, and proper-goal setting. Its relevance here lies in the fact that Dr. Maltz was neither a psychiatrist, nor a psychologist, but a plastic surgeon. He was inspired to develop this system of therapy because he saw so many patients who believed that a surgery altering their physical appearance would improve their quality of life but were bitterly disappointed. This has serious implications today for individuals considering surgeries to remove or alter their sexual organs.

Praying for Us Sinners

We can grow best in hating sin and loving sinners when we directly ask God for His help. Such requests are already present in many traditional Catholic prayers if we take the time to think about them carefully.

When we pray in the Our Father that God's will be done, we are praying that we and others will act in accordance with the natural law and God's law of love. When we ask forgiveness for our sins and promise to forgive the sins of others, we recognize that we, too, are sinners and we must love sinners while hating sin. When we ask God to lead us not into temptation and to deliver us from evil, we must recognize that *we* are to act as God's instruments on earth. We should play no role in tempting others to sin or in promoting evils.

The Blessed Mother is there to help us as well when we pray for her intercession in the Hail Mary. We ask her to "pray for us sinners, now and at the hour of our death." This should remind us that we are not only surrounded by sinners but are in their number. Further, we should act out against sin and for the benefit of sinners, so that, in keeping with our first and foremost life lesson, we might all come to see God face-to-face — and the Mother of God too!

We can also simply pray to God to give us the courage, charity, and wisdom to give fraternal correction when necessary, but always in a loving, prudent manner. In the words of the great Polish theologian St. John Cantius (1390–1473): "Fight all error, but do it with good humor, patience, kindness, and love. Harshness will damage your own soul and spoil the best cause."[65]

---

[65] As a university professor and theologian, St. John Cantius was a man after St. Thomas's heart, and as a physicist who helped

How the Sacraments Sever
Sin through Christ's Love

Let's conclude with a brief survey of a simple way that every one of the sacraments can help the cause of hating sin and loving sinners. Through the sacrament of *Baptism*, everyone on earth can potentially become a member of the Body of Christ and the Holy Catholic Church He established, thus opening the gates to potential fulfillment of life lesson number one of living in eternal bliss with God. May our Baptism recall our rejection of sin and inspire us to help reject sin in our culture to the spiritual benefit of all.

Confirmation strengthens us in all the graces God has bestowed upon us in Baptism, including the Holy Spirit's gift of spiritual strength — that of *fortitude*. If it is difficult for us to speak out in public against sin or privately to correct a brother, let us remember that we can always call upon this special strength of the Holy Spirit. (We'll spell this out much more clearly in our very next chapter.)

Through the sacrament of *Reconciliation*, there is hope for every one of us as a sinner. We should avail of it ourselves and encourage our loved ones, also sinners, to experience the relief and the joy it provides, reminding us that God always has mercy toward those who sincerely repent of their sins and strive to amend their lives. When we confess, we might consider whether we have been remiss in neglecting to offer fraternal correction or in receiving it poorly from others.

---

develop a theory of impetus, explaining the motion of projectiles against gravity, he was also a man after the heart of St. Thomas's great teacher, St. Albert the Great (ca. 1200–1280), the patron saint of scientists.

Those of us blessed with the sacrament of *Matrimony* should be thankful to God for how it sanctifies the sexuality of a man and a woman and opens it up to new life. We are also obliged to help each other get to heaven, which may at times involve administering (with utmost care!) spousal correction, if our spouse is doing something seriously sinful—and graciously submitting to it ourselves when we've done wrong!

Anointing of the Sick is also a remedy against sin and an act of love toward sinners. Whether or not God chooses to heal a physical ailment, this sacrament provides spiritual healing to all who are open to it.

The *Eucharist* should remind us of the ultimate act of hating (and conquering) sin while dearly loving sinners. We will ponder this Blessed Sacrament in more depth when we arrive at our final life lesson.

Holy Orders, for those chosen by God to receive it, becomes the source and font of *all* of the sacraments, through the priest who acts *in persona Christi*, "in the person of Christ." The priest has an awesome power and duty to hate sin in himself and in his flock, to speak out and act out against it, to heal and forgive it, and to provide us with the God-given sacramental graces to conquer sin and grow in love.

LIFE LESSON 7 SUMMA

We are truly called as followers of Christ to hate sin out of our love for sinners, including ourselves. God has given us the natural inborn capacities to ferret out fundamental natural laws of morality, and He has made His will in such matters entirely explicit through His revelation. We are called never to endorse sinful behaviors and sometimes to speak out against them, even when such behaviors have become politicized and glamorized in popular culture, while those who speak their consciences may be vilified or demonized. St. Thomas's nuanced writings on the corporal work of mercy of fraternal correction can aid us in the nuances of expressing our opposition to sinful behaviors in the right spirit, in the right manner, and at the right time, so that charity and justice are served. While our hearts must be filled with love for sinners, our intellects must also be open to the true causes and effects of sinful behaviors promoted in modern culture. We must pray for sinners, including ourselves, and recognize how every one of the sacraments can help us to conquer hateful sin and shower with love our neighbors and ourselves, so prone to sin when we reject God's law and His graces.

Be a Man (or a Woman)!

*God provides every one of us the strength
to stand up and do what's right.*

Question 8
How do we acquire the courage to stand up for what is right?

Thomas answers that …

"Fortitude, as a virtue, perfects the mind in the endurance of all perils whatever; but it does not go so far as to give confidence of overcoming all dangers: this belongs to the fortitude that is the gift of the Holy Spirit."

—*Summa Theologica* II-II, 139, 1

Toxic Masculinity, Anyone?
(or Perhaps Toxic Femininity?)

This chapter's life lesson examines how we as men or women can develop and express the spiritual strength we need to live upright lives in an exceptionally morally challenged culture. In Thomas's terms, the virtue that gives us the strength to overcome difficult obstacles to obtain moral goods is *fortitude*. The word derives from the Latin word *fortis*, for "strength," and it survives in other English words, for example, in the *fortified* (strengthened) buildings that we call, well, *forts*. In this chapter we'll focus on how we can fortify our souls.

We touched upon fortitude in earlier chapters—for example, when we looked at its relationship to *magnanimity*, or greatness of soul, in chapter 6, and its relationship to mustering the courage to provide and accept fraternal correction in chapter 7. Well, magnanimity is but one of four "integral parts" of fortitude per St. Thomas, and we'll meet the other three in this chapter's virtue section. Fortitude also applies to many situations besides fraternal correction, and we'll consider some of them in this chapter, but first, an unfortunate aside, courtesy of yet another recent example of the "toxic" (poisonous) culture of our turbulent times.

Manliness has long been a synonym for the bravery, courage, guts, ruggedness, or fortitude associated with *masculinity*, the qualities, attributes, and behaviors associated with being a male.[66] Who does not know that the admonishment to boys or men to "Be a man!" or "Man up!" means to stand up, be responsible, be strong, do what is difficult, and do the right thing? Just check any reputable dictionary for "manliness" and "masculinity," and you'll see what I mean.

Alas, we live in a day when dictionary definitions are being turned on their heads and many important words come to mean whatever powerful cultural forces would like them to mean, as we've seen, for example, in the redefinitions of "marriage" and "gender." So, too, go manliness and masculinity, which are even now referred to as "toxic" or poisonous.

---

[66] Thomas, in the thirteenth century, notes that Andronicus of Rhodes, a teacher of Aristotle's philosophy in the first century B.C., listed *manliness* as a virtue annexed to fortitude, and further, that "manliness is apparently the same as confidence, for he (Andronicus) says that *manliness is a habit of self-sufficiency in matters of virtue*" (II-II, 129).

A recent case in point was the American Psychological Association's August 2018 release of their *APA Guidelines for Psychological Practice with Boys and Men*. With noble stated aims of helping more males in need of psychological treatment seek out and obtain appropriate therapy, the document unquestionably treats what it calls "traditional masculinity" as a danger and treats masculinity in a completely different manner from which "femininity" was treated in their *2007 APA Guidelines for Psychological Practice with Girls and Women*. Indeed, a simple computer word check yields over seventy uses of the word "masculinity" and fifteen uses of the phrase "traditional masculinity" in the men's guidelines text, while the women's guideline text uses the term "femininity" merely one time, and the phrase "traditional femininity" not at all. Of further interest, the women's guidelines did not use the term "masculinity" in its text, while the men's guidelines use the term "femininity" once, and that in the context of attitudes of "anti-femininity." There is no reference to the ideal complementarity of masculinity and femininity. Further, the phrase "anti-masculinity" appears in neither document, though I would aver that the sentiment comes through quite clearly in the men and boys document!

The current APA guidelines note that boys and men are very much at risk for psychological disorders in our day, which is certainly true—as it is for women. They note that men may carry their need for strength and self-sufficiency too far, which can indeed be the case.[67] As Thomas himself would tell us, any virtue involves finding the mean between excess and deficiency, too much and too little. Indeed, as a *lack of fortitude* in men or

---

[67] Recall the relationship between *manliness*, *self-sufficiency*, and *confidence* in our previous footnote on Andronicus of Rhodes.

in women could lead them to seek too quickly outside help or medications for minor problems they can handle on their own with concerted effort, so, too, is *too great a reliance on one's own strength* an *excess* that merely mimics true fortitude. True fortitude recognizes not only one's strength, but *the limits* of one's strength too. Men may indeed be less likely to seek help when they really need it, and that is not fortitude but its excess, which is an improper fearlessness, temerity, or foolhardiness. Does "traditional masculinity" encourage such excess rather than true fortitude? The APA guidelines conclude that it does.

Great care must be used in examining the comparative mental health data for men and women, especially if "traditional masculinity" is to be portrayed as something negative and dangerous. In its 2019 "Continuing Education Corner" article on these guidelines, which APA members can read and be tested on to acquire continuing education credit, it clearly states the following: "The main thrust of the subsequent research is that traditional masculinity—marked by stoicism, competitiveness, dominance and aggression—is, on the whole, harmful."[68]

In one use of empirical data to buttress this idea of harmful traditional masculinity, data from the National Center for Health Statistics are cited that show, for example, a 28 percent increase in suicide rates for non-Hispanic white men in the years 1999 to 2014, truly a disturbing statistic that shows the sad state of our modern culture. The article also notes: "Suicide rates for women have been on the rise as well, but because men complete suicide more often than women, men's suicide death

---

[68] Stephanie Pappas, "APA Issues First-Ever Guidelines for Practice with Men and Boys," *Monitor on Psychology* 50, no. 1 (2019): 34, https://www.apa.org/monitor/2019/01/ce-corner.

rates remain the highest." It does *not* note two other relevant facts, however.

First, data has shown for decades that while men do *complete* fatal suicides at three to four times the rate of women, women *attempt* suicide at two to three times the rate of men. Women tend to use less fatal means than men, such as an overdose of medication as opposed to a gun. Clearly, suicide is a horrible problem in our day for both men and women. Second, a review of the National Center for Health Statistics' data for suicide rates from 1999 to 2014 shows that, as the APA reported, non-Hispanic white men's suicide rates indeed rose 28 percent (from 20.2 to 25.8 per 100,000), but non-Hispanic white women's suicide rates rose 60 percent (from 4.7 to 7.5 per 100,000), an increase in *women's* completed suicides *more than twice* the increase for men.

The bottom line is that these are trying times for both men and women. *One of the first things we need to do is to develop the strength of the virtue of fortitude, and the last thing we should do is pit men and women against one another, labeling either femininity or masculinity as toxic in itself.* Toxins are poisons that can destroy life, and it is, of course, only through the unity of the masculine and the feminine that human life can be produced.

If I might dip one last time into the APA's depiction of a harmful "traditional masculinity," I must note that that adjective "stoic" really jumped out at me as most ironic. The small-*s* stoic refers to the tendency to suppress one's emotions, especially common among men. I happen to have written a book on the big-*S* Stoics, so to speak, from whom we derive the small-*s* stoic adjective, the ancient Greek and later Roman Stoic philosophers. Their founder, Zeno (ca. 334–262 B.C.), originally taught under a famous *stoa* (porch) in Athens and this gave rise to their name "Stoics." Anyway, here are a couple of ironic twists.

12 Life Lessons from St. Thomas Aquinas

The most common and effective systems of "cognitive-behavioral therapies" in use in psychotherapy today are founded upon principles taught by those same ancient Stoics! Epictetus (A.D. 50–135) wrote, for example, that "it is not things themselves that disturb men, but their judgement about these things."[69] Psychologist Albert Ellis, Ph.D., noted that this insight from Epictetus, just as applicable to women as to men, formed the kernel of his own Rational Emotive Behavior Therapy. Indeed, it was Ellis's writings that first led me to the Stoics. Psychiatrist Aaron Beck, M.D., founder of Cognitive Therapy, acknowledges his debt to the Stoics as well. Such prominent Stoic-derived systems of modern psychotherapy strive not to suppress emotions but to bring emotions in line with healthy, realistic, rational thinking. And note well, this is also a fundamental attribute of virtue itself per St. Thomas Aquinas, wherein we come to bring our passions and desires under the guidance of right reason.

Further, a character we met in our last chapter was the Stoic philosopher Musonius Rufus, great champion of life and of natural law, who was Epictetus's teacher. Considering that "stoicism" is being used as one defining characteristic of a harmful traditional masculinity, one might be surprised to learn that Rufus was also among the most outspoken ancient thinkers regarding the dignity of—women! He taught that women had the same reasoning capacity and the same ability and need to acquire the same moral virtues as men do. Indeed, regarding courage or fortitude,[70] Rufus would write:

---

[69] Epictetus, *The Encheiridion* (Cambridge, MA: Harvard University Press, 2000), 487.

[70] Note that the Greek word that Rufus used for "bravery" was *andreia*, deriving from the word *andros*, meaning "a male." In

Perhaps someone might say that courage is a virtue appropriate to men only. That is not so. For a woman too of the right sort must have courage and be wholly free of cowardice, so that she will neither be swayed by hardships nor by fear; otherwise, how will she be said to have self-control, if by threat or force she can be constrained to yield to shame? Nay more, it is necessary for women to be able to repel attack, unless indeed they are willing to appear more cowardly than hens and other female birds which fight with creatures larger than themselves to defend their young.[71]

Clearly then, natural law itself dictates that both men and women develop the virtue of fortitude and express it in their lives. I cannot help but note again a corruption of natural law in our time. While Rufus observes the natural propensities of even birds to defend their offspring at the cost of their own lives, the most heated debates of our time involve the "right" of human mothers to kill their own children if those children are considered to bring an inconvenience into their lives. We certainly need courageous men and women to speak out and keep fighting the good fight for life as our culture slides back into barbarism, infanticide and all.

---

essence, he argued that women, too, need the "manly" virtue of "traditional masculinity"!

[71] Cora Lutz, *Musonius Rufus Fragments* (New Delhi, India: Isha Books, 2013), 14. Note that Christ also uses hens as an example when speaking of Jerusalem. He compares the way they protect their young to how He desires to protect the children of His people: "How often would I have gathered your children together as a hen gathers her brood under her wings, and you would not!" (Matt. 23:37; Luke 13:34).

12 Life Lessons from St. Thomas Aquinas

Even during St. Thomas's lifetime, in 1256 Pope Alexander IV sent Thomas's teacher St. Albert the Great and a small group of his peers to the far reaches of the frontier lands of Poland, Prussia, and Livonia in the office of papal legate. These previously Christianized lands had suffered repeated invasions from Tatars and Mongols and had restored many barbarous laws and brutal pagan customs. St. Albert was astonished by the degradations. And what were these horrible crimes? They slaughtered children born with deformities, since they would not be able to bear arms or serve their parents or their state; they determined the number of children each family could rear; they euthanized the elderly who were unfit for labor or service. Indeed, Albert noted they would proudly point out the graves of their own parents they had massacred, and he was outraged that they still called themselves Christians. Do you see any parallels in our turbulent times, with abortion, euthanasia, and even infanticide encouraged and applauded by people who still call themselves Catholics?[72]

---

[72] For details, see Joachim Sighart, *Albert the Great: His Life and Scholastic Labours: From Original Documents* (Charleston, SC: Bibilolife, 2009). Fr. Sighart (1824–1867) would write of the incident that "no one has rights over his fellow-creature as though he were no more than a mere brute—such crimes ought naturally to excite horror" (p. 166). Little did he know that in the years ahead, such "rights" would be found in the constitutions of many nations, and for some, the natural horror at such deeds would be replaced by triumphant public celebrations. Why are not manly bishops in our day taking stronger actions to condemn such deeds and safeguard human life? And let's not go the "seamless garment" route and consider the pro-life cause simply one of many issues of comparable concern. It is certainly impossible to wear any kind of seamless garment, particularly a diaper, if one's body has been destroyed.

Of course, Thomas knew well, according to the teachings of Scripture and the Catholic Church, that men and women are equal in dignity in God's eyes. In commenting on Genesis 2:22 on God's crafting of Eve from Adam's rib, Thomas recognized the importance of the symbolic meaning of the passage. He notes that woman was not described as being made from man's head, because she was not to rule over him. She was not made from his feet, because neither was she to be held in contempt as his slave. She was made from his rib to signify their *social union*. "Secondly, for the sacramental signification; for from the side of Christ sleeping on the Cross, the sacraments flowed — namely, blood and water — on which the Church was established" (I, 92, 3). True masculinity and true femininity, which develop all the virtues God gave us as men or women, are anything but toxic; indeed, they are holy.

Every Evil Is a Weakness

Thomas tells us that whereas "virtue implies a perfection of power ... every evil is a weakness" (I-II, 55, 3). All virtues perfect the various powers within us, as *prudence*, for example, perfects our practical reasoning powers to find the right means to virtuous ends, *justice* perfects the capacity of our will to give each person his rightful due, and *temperance* perfects the power of our reason to rein in our sensual desires when they would produce harm. The same applies to the virtue of *fortitude*, since it perfects the power of our reason to rein in our fears and prompts us to action in the face of difficult evils.

Fortitude, however, implies *power* in another very specific sense, since it is the virtue of *strength* itself. This is why fortitude is also known as the "guardian of the virtues." Fortitude can give us the strength to stick to prudent moral actions in the face of outside pressures, perhaps pressures to lie in order to further a cause, since, as so many seem to think, "the end justifies the means." Fortitude can give us the strength to treat every individual justly, even when society might pressure us to treat others differently due to the color of their skin in light of past "oppressions" or current "privilege." Fortitude can give us strength to rein in our passions for illicit pleasures, such as nonmarital "consensual" sex of any manner or cannabinoid drugs, while our lawmakers struggle to find ever more new ways to lead us into such temptations.[73]

There is a sense then in which every vice is a weakness, a tendency to fail to develop or exercise the virtue of fortitude. Hence, if we are to grow in fortitude, we would do well indeed to declare ourselves mortal enemies of every mortal vice that may be festering in our souls. Still, Thomas and many Church Fathers before him have also warned us *of a vice that is specifically characterized by spiritual weakness*, making it a weak and yet deadly foe of both the spiritual strength that is *fortitude* and the greatness of soul that is fortitude's ally of *magnanimity*. Standing (or slouching, rather) directly opposite the virtue of magnanimity is the vice of *pusillanimity* (which derives from the Latin word *pusillus*, meaning "very little," "petty," or "paltry"). Let's hear Thomas on the matter:

---

[73] As I write, on February 21, 2019, my local newspaper's front-page headline details our governor's plan to ease Illinois's fiscal problems through the legalization of marijuana and "sports wagering" — governmentally endorsed drug use and gambling to the rescue of the public good! (As I review this on June 30, 2019, the recreational drug law has been passed and the gambling law is imminent.)

Pusillanimity makes a man fall short of what is proportionate to his power.... Hence it is that the servant who buried in the earth the money that he received from his master, and did not trade with it through fainthearted fear, was punished by his master. (II-II, 133, 1)

Pusillanimity is a "fainthearted fear" that short-circuits our potential to do the good for our own, our neighbor's, and our heavenly Master's benefits. While the pride-driven vice of *presumption* overestimates our own powers, *pusillanimity* grossly underestimates the powers God has given us, and indeed, pride, that "queen of the vices," may even play a role in pusillanimity. Per Thomas: "Even pusillanimity may in some way be the result of pride; when, to wit, a man clings too much to his own opinion, whereby he thinks himself incompetent for those things for which he is competent" (II-II, 133, 1). Fainthearted smallness of soul may bespeak a false, prideful humility.

Sadly, there are many cultural forces in our day that work to foster smallness of soul in both men and women. Some cultural critics bewail the emasculation of many young men, sometimes called "man-boys" according to prominent psychologists Philip Zimbardo and Nikita Coulombe in their *The Demise of Guys: Why Boys Are Struggling and What We Can Do about It.* There are growing numbers of men who delay forming serious relationships, getting married, getting a job, or even setting down their video game controls to search for a home outside their parents' basements. At the same time, many young women wonder where manly gentleman have gone, and the lament is far from limited to devout Catholics.

Just two days ago, as I sat awaiting an eye doctor's appointment, a popular national daytime television show blared a few feet above my suffering ears. An attractive young woman lamented to the popular host that the men she goes out with expect physical affection from her from the start of the first date, before they have even begun to know each other. She wondered where young men have learned to take women for granted and treat them so poorly.

Well, our popular culture clearly promotes petty pusillanimity in men, encouraging them to seek out simple sexual pleasures whenever possible, especially since any unwanted effects of sexual union can easily be contracepted by a variety of means, or simply aborted if all else fails. After all, the call for unlimited "reproductive health" rights for women is an incredibly powerful inducement to men's treatment of women as sexual objects, rather than potential body and soul mates for life. I was pleasantly surprised to hear the host on the television show reply to his guest that women have the capacity to train men how to treat them, by respecting and rewarding only truly manly, gentlemanly behavior. Indeed, a small-souled male is unlikely to think much about the soul and the dignity of a potential romantic partner unless she lets him know that he needs to "Man up!"

Note, too, how Thomas refers to the lesson Christ taught us about the dire effects of pusillanimity in the parable of the master and the talents (Matt. 25:14–30). The master greatly rewarded the servant who, through his efforts, turned the five talents[74] he had given him into ten, and he welcomed him into his joy. He did the same thing for the servant who turned his two talents

---

[74] A talent was a sizable sum of money, worth more than fifteen years' wages for a laborer in those times. For the ancient Greeks, a talent of silver was the amount required to outfit one complete ship of war.

into four. On the contrary, to the servant who did nothing to multiply the one talent he had been given, but merely buried it in the ground, the master took his talent and gave it to the man with ten talents, casting the pusillanimous servant "into the outer darkness."

Perhaps a harsh lesson, but the parable makes clear that the master originally gave to each man *according to his ability* and expected each man to make the most of it. He was as pleased with the man who turned two talents into four as he was with the man who turned five into ten. Surely, he would have been equally pleased if the less-gifted man with one talent did what he could to turn his one into two. Let us see here the lesson of how, through pusillanimity, we sell ourselves short, underestimating our own potentials and thereby failing to strive to develop them to their fullest, regardless of how they might compare with the potentials and results of our neighbors.

So then, if we are to practice the life lesson of being a man or a woman, of having the strength to stand up for what is right, we will need to recognize pusillanimity when we see it raise its fearful head in ourselves, and strive to pulverize its soul-shrinking effects.

Fortitude and Its Four Stalwart Parts

To stand up for what is right, we must know that there *is* a right in the first place! This will take not only the kind of true knowledge St. Thomas teaches but also true fortitude in a culture so rampant with the *moral relativism* that denies there are any absolute rights and wrongs, and the philosophical *constructivism* that proposes that truth is not a correspondence between our thoughts and external reality, but that we "construct truths" based on our desires and needs. This is why some now think it sane for a person to "identify" as a woman if he is a man, or as a "person of color,"

if he, she (or "X" or "ze" as some prominent politicians are lob-
bying for) is, in fact, a Caucasian. We used to have a different
approach when people's identities did not match up to external
realities. We called these thoughts "delusions" and tried to help
people who thought they were Napoleon or Christ, for example,
rather than agreeing they were correct and mandating by law
that others proclaim they agree with them too!

As for the virtue of fortitude, Thomas notes that it has two
positive essential, integral parts": the virtues of *magnanimity* and of
magnificence. "Magnificence" derives from the Latin words *magnus*
("great," as we have seen with "magnanimity") and *facere*, "to
make or do." The virtue of magnificence, then, is about making
great things, and this specifically entails the proper expendi-
ture of money. *Through fortitude we overcome fear of threats to our
body, while through magnificence we overcome fear of threats to our
pocketbooks.* Consider if you will, the incredible outlay of money
and effort made by entire communities to erect the magnificent
European cathedrals and basilicas of the Middle Ages. Its contrary vices are *meanness* or stinginess on the side of deficiency
and *wastefulness* on the side of excess.

Can you think of a scriptural example of a tale of magnificence? How about the parable of the master and the servants
again? Recall that every servant was given a magnificent sum of
money, and each was expected to make something great of it, to
the best of his ability. Two of the servants did so magnificently,
according to their abilities.

Fortitude also has two "enduring parts." Indeed, per Thomas:
"Now the principal act of fortitude is to endure" (II-II, 123, 6).
While *magnanimity* and *magnificence* strive to achieve difficult
goals and produce great things, *patience* and *perseverance* enable
us "to stand immovable in the midst of dangers" (ibid.).

Patientia is Latin for the ability to endure suffering, and patience, as a part of fortitude, describes our ability to endure suffering without becoming sorrowful or defeated. Patience also implies an ability to endure suffering produced from the outside, from the acts of another. If you have ever told someone, "You have the patience of a saint!" chances are the saintlike one has endured with calmness and grace the annoying and bothersome behavior of another person, perhaps complaints, disrespect, or ingratitude from the very one he or she was trying to help. In a mystical experience, God said to St. Catherine of Siena that "a man proves his patience on his neighbor, when he receives injuries from him."[75] St. Catherine knew well that those who acquire the virtue of patience will not melt when confronted like the "snowflakes" of our day, but will stand firm and fast when the going gets tough — even if (heaven forbid), someone makes a statement with which they disagree!

Further, when we seek virtuous goods, we must often bide our time. Many pleasures come quickly and easily, whereas virtuous rewards may be a long time in the making, sometimes even a lifetime. It is patience that enables us to do the right things with gladness in our hearts, while we endure present evils, patient for true goods that lie ahead.

And speaking of time, *perseverance* is a special virtue of fortitude that enables us to endure to the end in virtuous acts, regardless of delays. For a soldier, this might mean displaying the fortitude to stand his ground until the end of a long, drawn-out battle. To the magnificent person, this might mean staying the course and providing whatever additional funds are needed to fund a great public work beset with unexpected delays or expenses. To

[75] *Dialogue* 17.

the student, perseverance may mean continuing to study until ready for the exam, even as the lure of the television or the mattress grow ever more enticing.

Perseverance moderates or controls our passions, such as fear of weariness or failure in the face of delays. The vice of deficiency in relation to perseverance carries the name of *effeminacy* (but in no way implies that women cannot display perseverance — as we know for a fact that so many women saints have persevered remarkably well, despite the most trying obstacles and delays). Effeminacy refers to an inability to suffer hardship or toil due to an inordinate love of pleasure, play, or leisure. You've heard the saying "When the going gets tough, the tough get going." Well, when the going gets tough, the effeminate get going too, to look for something easier to do, such as going along with the crowd! The effeminate individual has trained himself toward weakness and delicacy. He has buried his talent for manly perseverance deep in the ground, where it may rest in peace but fail to grow.

In the grandest sense of all, perseverance is intricately related to the lifelong practice of our very first life lessons, for "he who endures to the end will be saved" (Matt. 24:13). This brings us to a consideration of the ultimate act of fortitude.

St. Thomas tells us that *martyrdom* is the extreme example of the virtue of fortitude in action. Fortitude is the virtue that enables us to conquer our fears in order to stay the course and stand up for what we know is right, for what we know to be true and good. Thomas tells us that while "out of the love of God, we ought to love our bodies also" (II-II, 25, 5), "the brave man has a stronger love for the good of virtue than for his own body" (ibid., 123, 8). Remember that the irascible appetite enables us to fight against that which deprives us of the good things that we love and desire. And note as well that the irascible appetite strives after "arduous" or "difficult" goods, good actions that may cause us great discomfort, and in thankfully rare cases, even death. Further, "it belongs to the virtue of fortitude to remove any obstacle that withdraws the will from following reason" (II-II, 123, 3). The martyr, male or female, sees fidelity to God as the ultimate good, and this supreme fortitude allows the martyr to fight against the evil that would ensue if he or she allowed aversion to pain to conquer the will to follow God.

Thankfully, few of us today will ever have to face the supreme test of the virtue of fortitude,[76] but bear well in mind that "he that stands firm against great things, will in consequence stand firm against less things" (II-II, 123, 4). In other words, when we have developed the virtue of fortitude fit to confront great and arduous tasks, we will be all the more up to the task of those smaller, though difficult virtuous deeds in our daily lives, whether it be speaking up for our beliefs,[77] enduring physical fatigue when

---

[76] Though indeed, it still does happen, as Christians are sometimes martyred in the Middle East today. In 2016, a French priest was martyred while saying Mass. And sadly, it happens even in the United States, where, in 2018, an American woman suffered martyrdom in a Catholic bookstore in St. Louis, Missouri, refusing to comply with the depraved requests of an armed gunman before he shot her to death. Talk about turbulent times. God rest these valiant souls.

[77] Note well that "silence" is one of at least nine ways we cooperate in another's sin, and therefore join that person in sin. The other ways include cooperation through counsel, command, consent, provocation, praise or flattery, concealment, partaking, and defense of sinful action. See CCC 1868 and Angelo Stagnaro, "9 Ways You Might Be Sharing in the Sins of Others," *National*

helping out a friend with some task, or studying and praying instead of vegetating in front of the television.

The Power of Praying for Power

The first prayer that comes to my mind when I think of fortitude is that simple, oft-heard prayer, "Lord, give me strength!" In fact, there is nothing at all wrong with short, sweet prayers like that to call upon God when we face life's difficulties and could use some instantaneous spiritual fortification to help us "Man up!" or indeed, "Woman up!," as the case may be. St. Alphonsus Liguori (1696–1787) has crafted a nice petition to God for fortitude: "Grant me the spirit of fortitude that I may bear my cross with Thee, and that I may overcome with courage all the obstacles that oppose my salvation."[78]

St. Thomas and his wise Franciscan colleague St. Bonaventure concur that the petition in the Our Father "give us this day our daily bread" pertains to the Holy Spirit's gift of fortitude.[79] Bonaventure explains that this is because bread "strengthens the human heart,"[80] echoing Psalm 104 [103]:15, and Thomas chimes in that "this gift of fortitude prevents man's heart from fainting through fear of lacking necessities, and makes him trust without

---

Catholic Register, June 13, 2017, http://www.ncregister.com/blog/astagnaro/9-ways-you-might-be-sharing-in-the-sins-of-others.

[78] This is part of his "Prayer for the Gifts of the Holy Spirit," available in various translations online.

[79] Bear with me for just a minute, if you will. In our next section, we'll address the important distinction between the *virtue* and the *gift* of fortitude.

[80] St. Bonaventure, *Collations on the Seven Gifts of the Holy Spirit*, trans. Zachary Hayes, O.F.M. (St. Bonaventure, NY: Franciscan Institute Publications, 2008), 49.

wavering that God will provide him with whatever we need. For this reason the Holy Spirit, the giver of this fortitude, teaches us to pray to God to *give us this day our daily bread.*"[81]

As for a prayer that speaks to and reminds us of the most heavenly heights of both masculinity and femininity, I can recommend none more highly than the Holy Rosary, whereby, through the intercession of that "new Eve," the Blessed Mother, God's masterwork of the feminine, we meditate on the life and the lessons of the "new Adam," the very Son of God and the epitome of masculine holiness.

Sacrament of Strength

After addressing the *virtue* of fortitude with remarkable thoroughness in a full twelve articles in the *Summa Theologica* (II-II, 123), Thomas addresses in two additional articles the *gift* of fortitude and just how it differs from the virtue,[82] and here he explains precisely how the gift of fortitude further fortifies the virtue. We have seen that the natural virtue of fortitude is a "firmness of mind" that allows us to do good and endure what is evil, especially when our actions involve things that are arduous or difficult. Man does possess the capacity to exercise such firmness, both in accomplishing arduous goods and in enduring "grievous evil," and this is the stuff of the virtue of fortitude.

The *gift* of fortitude, however, through the guidance of the Holy Spirit, allows man *not only to struggle to achieve* his ends despite difficulties, but *to achieve his final end.* Through virtuous acts of fortitude, perhaps to defend one's loved ones or country,

---

[81]   *Aquinas Catechism*, 137.

[82]   Ibid., Q. 139, "Of the Gift of Fortitude." (Subsequent citations in this section come from this question's first article.)

a person might well be thwarted by death, but through the Holy Spirit's gift of fortitude, that person can overcome even death and achieve his final ultimate end of everlasting life with God in heaven. Further, the gift will infuse within one's mind "a certain confidence" that will dispel the most powerful fears, as we see in the cases of the holy martyrs who cherish the gift of fortitude more than even their own bodies.

While none of the seven sacraments is named fortitude, one has a particularly powerful link to the gift of fortitude, and this is the sacrament of Confirmation, whereby our faith is made firm and strong. St. Thomas wrote that "Confirmation is to Baptism as growth is to birth" (III, 72, 6), and as we grow bigger, we grow stronger. The *Catechism* tells us "by the sacrament of Confirmation, [the baptized] are more perfectly bound to the Church and are enriched with a special strength of the Holy Spirit" (1285). While the sacrament strengthens us in all of the gifts of the Holy Spirit, again, it provides us with a special strength of the Holy Spirit to spread and defend the faith (CCC 1303).

As for the minister of this sacrament, it is the bishop who lays hands on the recipient, anoints the recipient with chrism, and pronounces the words of the rite of Confirmation, invoking the spiritual seal of the Holy Spirit. Why the bishop for Confirmation, while priests administer Baptism? "Though he who is baptized is made a member of the Church, nevertheless he is not yet enrolled as a Christian solider. And therefore he is brought to the bishop, as to the commander of the army" (III, 72, 10). Just look at today's headlines: you cannot ignore the fact that the Church is indeed under attack by a variety of secular forces, and Christians in parts of the world are being attacked, driven from their lands, and even martyred in numbers unseen for hundreds of years. Sadly, the Church is also under attack from some elements within in it. Indeed, we all need to "put on the whole armor of God" (see Eph. 6:13), and "fight the good fight of the faith" (1 Tim. 6:12) in ways we may not have imagined even a few years ago. Lord, give us the strength of the gift of fortitude!

There is another sacrament that can fortify us, too, in a most special way. Every time we receive the Eucharist, we receive the most powerful "daily bread" in all of creation: the Body, Blood, Soul, and Divinity of Him through whom all things were made (see John 1:3).

Life Lesson 8 Summa

We must remember that God crafted us male and female. So, be a man (or a woman) as God has created you. It is a very good thing for men to be manly and women to be womanly, and only through their union does new life come forth. We must educate ourselves about the strengths and gifts of both sexes and grow in those that we share, lifting each other up. We must reject the pusillanimity, or smallness of soul, that would declare masculinity or femininity "toxic" instead of live-giving. We must grow in the virtue of fortitude and pray for all of its positive and enduring allied virtues of magnanimity, magnificence, patience, and perseverance, so that we may continue to seek and work for great goods while enduring hardships and evils over the long run, knowing that with the Holy Spirit's gift of fortitude, strengthened in the sacrament of Confirmation, we can finally achieve the ultimate prize in heaven.

Go to Mass, Not to the Woods, Every Sunday

Because we are bodily and spiritual beings, we must be religious too.

Question 9
Why can't we just be spiritual but not religious?

Thomas answers that ...

"A man is said to be religious from 'religio,' because he often ponders over, and, as it were, reads again (religit), the things which pertain to worship. . . . Or again, religion may be derived from 'religare,' (to bind together) wherefore Augustine says (Of True Religion, 55): 'May religion bind us to the one Almighty God.'"

— *Summa Theologica* II-II, 81, 1

Keeping the Lord's Day Holy

The idea that we can, and indeed, should, be "spiritual but not religious" has become so popular in recent decades that it has acquired its own acronym (SBNR), or indeed, two of them if we include SBNA, "spiritual but not affiliated." The gist of the notion is an emphasis on the interior, *spiritual* experience of the individual, without the ostensibly unnecessary baggage of the exterior, communal, institutional dimensions of formal *religion*. Why go to church, "spiritual" people ask, when one can go to the woods and commune directly with God, or perhaps with the "god" who is one's own self?

Now, as with so many errors, there are some grains of truth here. We should indeed grow in our awareness of the importance of the spiritual, rather than becoming mired in the rampant materialism and consumerism so centered on worldly desires. In this sense, the idea bears a faint resemblance to our second life lesson, that we should focus the most on the things that matter the most, and to our sixth life lesson, that we should love what is highest within ourselves. Further, the man or woman who seeks God in the woods will indeed find Him there in some very important ways. As St. Thomas explains:

> God is in all things by His *power* inasmuch as all things are subject to his power: He is by His *presence* in all things, as all things are bare and open to His eyes; He is in all things by His *essence*, inasmuch as He is present to all as the cause of their being. (I, 8, 3, emphasis added)

As we read in Scripture: "Do I not fill heaven and earth? says the LORD" (Jer. 23:24). What we see in the woods or in the stars does indeed tell us something about God, for those who have eyes to see and ears to listen: "For from the greatness and beauty of created things comes a corresponding perception of their Creator" (Wisd. 13:5). Further, "the heavens are telling of the glory of God; and the firmament proclaims his handiwork" (Ps. 19:1). This is why Thomas's teacher St. Albert would joyously exclaim as both scientist and theologian: "The whole world is theology for us because the heavens proclaim the glory of God."[83]

---

[83] From St. Albert's *Commentary on St. Matthew*, as cited by Paul Murray, *The New Wine of Dominican Spirituality: A Drink Called Happiness* (New York: Burns and Oates, 2006), 93.

So, if you are inclined to praise God in the woods on Sunday, please, by all means do so—put in a good word for me if you think of it—but please do so *before* or *after* Mass.[84] And here's why.

St. Thomas went to great lengths to show us that our natural reason, starting with the simple evidence of our senses—the fact that things move or change, act as causes and are acted upon as effects, exist, have beauty, goodness, and order—can indeed lead us through incontrovertibly sound reasoning to the existence of the unmoved mover, first cause, necessarily existent, totally beautiful, good, and purposeful Being who is God.[85] Therefore, even through the power of reason alone, we should recognize that nature, however grand and beautiful, let alone our own souls, is not worthy of worship, but should point us to God alone, who is worthy of worship, for everything in the universe depends for its very creation *and* sustained existence on the power and love of God. God is not the universe, as pantheists proclaim, and, as G. K. Chesterton has reminded us, strictly speaking, nature is not our *mother*, but our *sister*. We owe her honor and proper stewardship, but not the worship due only to God.

According to St. Thomas, *what we can know about God through reason alone* is extremely valuable, though quite limited. We can know, for example, that He exists, that He is utterly simple (not composed of parts), perfect, infinite, immutable (unchangeable), one (a unity), supremely good and loving, immense (everywhere through essence, presence, and power), and eternal (I, 1-26).

---

[84] In unusual circumstances, Mass can be offered outside of a Church, including open-air services, but this is clearly the exception, and not the rule. (Thomas, who seems to address just about everything, addresses this in III, 83, 3.)

[85] See I, 2, 3 for his brief summary of five ways God's existence can be proven through reason.

These reasoned conclusions, however, are but *praeambula fidei*, "preambles of faith," that "remove obstacles to faith, by showing that what faith proposes is not impossible" (II-II, 2, 10).

Indeed, they removed such obstacles for me after twenty-five years of atheism, having been influenced by atheistic philosophers who had not grasped the philosophical and theological lessons of St. Thomas. Thomas showed, like no one before him or since, how not only reason, but *faith* is quite reasonable, never contradicting reason, but through the special revelation of God, the source and summit of Truth, transcending its human limitations in the most important ways.[86]

To make a very long story short, one of the most profound "Ahas!" to hit me after moving from the "god of the philosophers" provable by those preambles to the "God of Abraham, Isaac, and Jacob" (Exod. 3:15; Acts 7:32) was reading Thomas's elegant, extensive, metaphysically astute proofs of the existence of God, built upon but transcending the foundations of Aristotle, the Father of Logic, that show how in God and God alone in all the universe, *essence* and *existence, what He is* and *that He is* must be *one.* This cannot be said of you or of me, or of anything else that exists. I don't know your age, but I hadn't even begun forming in my mother's womb until 1960. The universe obviously existed quite a long time without me, but even the universe could not

---

[86] In the words of twentieth-century Thomist philosopher Etienne Gilson on the relationship between faith, reason, God's revelation, and the science of theology as a whole: "The theology of the Christian Doctors is only revelation investigated by reason working in the light of faith" *The Christian Philosophy of St. Thomas Aquinas* (Notre Dame, IN: University of Notre Dame Press, 1994), 94.

have created or sustained itself unless through the act of a Being who is completely *necessary*.

Now, as for the "Aha!": I also found in Thomas's arguments (in fact, he begins the *On the Contrary* section of I, 2, 3 with it), the tersest of all summaries of the argument—in the words of God Himself! When Moses asked God what he should call Him, God responded, "I AM WHO AM" (Exod. 3:14).

How amazing that what some would consider an ancient, simple, philosophically unsophisticated, superstitious desert people received from God the gist of this most profound argument in less than a handful of words. Indeed, before identifying Himself as the God of Abraham, Isaac, and Jacob, God instructed Moses: "Say this to the people of Israel, 'I AM has sent me to you'" (Exod. 3:14).

Well, "I AM," of course, had much more to tell Moses through His special revelation in the burning bush. Indeed, they include what we might call the most profound, important, and famous, ten "life lessons" of them all. I refer to the Ten Commandments, of course. Let's note that the first three pertain directly to man's relationship with God, and the other seven with man's relationship to himself and his neighbor. The first commandment bids us to honor God alone and no false idols, the second bids us not to use God's name in vain, and the third bids us to keep Holy the Sabbath Day.[87] Those first three are foremost and are interrelated, and the third directly prescribes the subject matter of this chapter's life lesson from St. Thomas Aquinas.

The Catholic Church, established by the Son of God and built upon the "rock" of the first pope, St. Peter (Matt.16:18),

---

[87] See Gen. 20:2–17, Deut. 5:6–21, and the CCC table between 2051 and 2052 for lists of the Ten Commandments.

has provided the most exalted of all ways to keep holy the Lord's Day in the form of the Holy Mass. We must strive to conquer sins and build virtues to appreciate fully this great gift, and to enjoy fully the effects of the sacrament it presents us, for in the Mass, God is present to us in the most special of all ways, in a more profound, intimate, and mystical way than even through His eternal presence, essence, and power. For now, let's turn our eyes toward the kinds of sins that turn our eyes away from God for the sake of infinitely lesser goods.

A Sin That May Be Spiritual, but Certainly Not Religious

We already encountered one major sin that opposes this chapter's life lesson, as a sin opposing the greatest of all commandments: to love God with all that we are. Thomas made clear: "Sloth is not an aversion of the mind from any spiritual good, but from the Divine good, to which the mind is obliged to adhere" (II-II, 35, 3). When *sloth* turns our minds away from God, it also gets busy turning our actions away from God, including the neglect of specific acts that God bids us to do: "Sloth is opposed to the precept about hallowing the Sabbath Day. For this precept, in so far as it is a moral precept, implicitly commands the mind to rest in God; and sorrow about the Divine good is contrary thereto" (ibid.). If we willingly fail to do honor to God in Mass on Sundays in keeping with the Catholic Church's teaching that it is a mortal sin in violation of the third commandment, then we know there is a *sloth* lurking lazily in our souls, and we need to take action to move it out, slowly, but surely!

Ignorance is another possible source of sin, when we lack knowledge regarding things every person is obliged to know. Thomas elaborates: "All are bound in common to know the articles of faith, and the universal principles of right" (I-II, 76, 2). If we fail to attend Sunday Mass because we have not bothered to learn the Church's teaching on how it relates to the third commandment, we have culpably sinned through ignorance. Perhaps, too, those who have not learned the difference between the woods and the church, which makes all the difference in the world—namely, the Real Presence of Christ in the Eucharist at Mass—have been negligent in learning the fundamentals of their Faith. Culpable, too, are ordained clerics who do not strive to dispel such ignorance in their own parishioners by explaining the Real Presence and displaying their awe in its reality through the reverent manner in which Mass is said.

Among modern errors that contribute to the "spiritual but not religious" misconception are the stated or implicit *pantheism* that sees God in everything in such a way that it does not distinguish creation from the Creator and the *modernism* that emphasizes religion as merely a matter of personal feeling or experience, rather than objective facts and the revealed truths of the Faith.

The Virtue of Being *Religious* and Not Merely Spiritual

To truly honor God in ways He intended, we must cultivate in our souls the *virtue* of *religion*. It is quite telling that in the "On the contrary" section of his first of eight articles on the virtue of religion, Thomas cites a non-Christian source, the pagan Roman philosopher, Marcus Tullius Cicero: "Tully says (*Rhetoric* 2, 53) that religion consists in offering service and ceremonial rites to a superior nature that men call divine" (II-II, 81, 1). This tells us that engrained in our human nature is the tendency to reason our way to the existence of some kind of divine being (or beings) and that such a being or beings are worthy of our worship and service.

Of course, Thomas also calls on the testimony of Scripture and the Church Fathers, including St. Augustine, to answer fully this first question of II-II, 81, on whether the virtue of religion directs man to *God alone*. Thomas ultimately answers this question with a resounding yes and provides all kinds of illumination along the way, shining light in particular on the idea of *latria*.

An *objection* in the first article notes that *latria* pertains to religion. Augustine said that *latria* means "service," and we are bound by charity to serve not only God but also our neighbor (see Gal. 5:13). Therefore, religion is also directed toward one's neighbor. Thomas responds, however, as follows:

> Since servant implies relation to a lord, wherever there is a special kind of lordship there must needs be a special kind of service. Now it is evident that lordship belongs to God in a special and singular way, because He made all things and has supreme dominion over all. Consequently a special kind of service is due to Him, which is known as *latria* in Greek; and therefore it belongs to religion. (II-II, 81, 1)

In sum, we owe to God a special kind of service we owe to no other being in the universe, or to the entire universe itself, and this we call *latria*, more commonly known today as *worship* or *adoration*. Recall, if you will, that in our treatment of *justice*, we briefly touched on *religion*. Thomas considered religion just a part of the cardinal virtue of justice because we can never exercise complete justice to God in returning to Him his due *in equal measure*: we owe Him everything that we are, including our very existence! Of course, God is quite aware of this situation and asks of us only what we are able to give back to Him, with the aid of His divine assistance! Because religion's object or end is God, though it is not one of the four cardinal moral virtues, "religion excels among the moral virtues," being the highest and most important among them. Further, "the precepts pertaining to religion are given precedence (Exod. 20) as being of greatest importance.... Therefore religion is the chief of the moral virtues" (II-II, 81, 6). The first through third commandments, directed toward God, command exercise of the virtue of religion.

Obviously, then, we would be especially wise to try to dispel any sinful ignorance within us by learning how to develop the virtue of religion in our souls. Of course, Thomas is always most happy to guide us along the way.

Recall, if you will, that our quotation that started this chapter noted that *religion* derives from the Latin word *relegit*, "to read again." St. Augustine noted religion's relation to the Latin word *religare*, "to bind together." St. Thomas notes that, in practicing the virtue of religion, we do read again and again the Scriptures and ponder again and again divine truths. The acts of religion confirm our bond to God. Indeed, he points out how both aspects of religion are made clear in the lives of the religious who are formally consecrated to God. Yet the religious and Christian laity alike are expected to develop the virtue of religion.

Let's remember that "a virtue is that which makes its possessor good, and his acts good likewise" (II-II, 81, 3). The virtue of religion then, entails both *interior* and *exterior acts*. It perfects our wills by directing them to God, but it *begins* through the operations of our *intellects*, as we ponder and pay homage to God's greatness, and it *ends* in outward *actions, directly* in our acts of worship to God, and *indirectly* in the good deeds we perform for our neighbors, as God would have us do. The virtue of religion itself, we might well say, declares itself "both spiritual and religious!"

Interior acts of religion include *devotion* and *prayer*. Devotion implies that we have "vowed" ourselves to God and dedicated our heart to live for Him. Prayer is the other essential interior act of religion, and we'll look at prayer in the light of St. Thomas's wisdom in our next section.

As for the *external* acts of religion, St. Thomas addresses in depth a variety of actions, including *adoration, sacrifice, oblations and first fruits, tithes, oaths,* and *vows*. We'll shed Thomas's light on these external acts in this chapter's last section, on the rite of the sacrament that perfects all of religion's interior and exterior acts.

Before we finish our virtue section for this life lesson, I'd not be surprised at all if at least one reader has scratched his or her venerable head, wondering when I'm going to get to how the theological virtue of *faith* relates to religion and the life lesson of this chapter. Well, good question (and well-warranted head scratch)! Thomas addressed the question of religion's relationship to faith in the fifth article of II-II, 81: "Whether Religion Is a Theological Virtue." His answer was no, and therein he explained how *religion* is a *moral* virtue that is guided by the even higher, God-infused *theological* virtue of *faith*, as well as hope and charity. Citing St. Augustine, he notes that "God is worshipped by faith, hope, and charity." Thomas notes that religion directs the acts that serve as the *means* directed toward the end of worshipping and showing reverence to God, while faith, hope, and charity directly serve the *end* of worshipping God by commanding those acts of religion. In another comparison of religion and faith in the same article, Thomas explains how supernatural faith transcends the limits of the moral virtue of religion:

> And yet the acts whereby God is worshipped do not reach out to God himself, as when we believe God we reach out

to Him by believing; for which reason it was stated (Q. 1, 1, 2, 4) that God is the object of faith, *not only because we believe in a God, but because we believe God.* (emphasis added)

Note well the subtlety of that last line. The virtue of faith does indeed go further than religion alone in providing an intimate, supernatural, personal relationship with God. We will examine it more thoroughly when we come to our last chapter, on the Person to whom faith, like religion, binds us, in the most glorious ways.

The Ultimate Place for Prayer

If your concept of prayer is a little vague or fuzzy, it won't be if you ever open the *Summa Theologica* itself and ponder the seventeen articles the Angelic Doctor devotes to the subject in II-II, 83. You will learn, for example, whether we should pray only directly to God, whether we should ask for specific things, and if so, if these include temporal or worldly things, why we should pray for others and for our enemies, why the seven petitions of the Lord's Prayer are "perfect," whether prayer is proper for a "rational being" (listen up, any modern thinkers who hold to the "science versus religion" false dichotomy!), whether we should pray out loud, whether we must pay attention while we pray (not always!), whether God hears the prayers of sinners, and whether the proper parts of prayer are supplications, prayers, intercessions, and thanksgivings.

Whew! There's quite a science to prayer, you see, and the Angelic Doctor is the master scientist. As usual, part of the reason St. Thomas knew so much was that he studied so extensively the great Fathers and Doctors before him. Just for a small sample of highlights: on prayers for others, which we have already seen in the context of other life lessons, he quotes the great Eastern Doctor St. John Chrysostom, who noted that prayer for ourselves comes from *necessity*, and prayer for others from *fraternal* (brotherly) *charity*, and "the prayer that comes from fraternal charity is sweeter to God than that which comes out of necessity." Further, as St. Isidore pointed out so wisely, "We say 'Our Father' and not 'My Father,' 'Give us' and not 'Give me.'"

Now, I'd like to ask if you can think of a place where we find virtually all of the most fundamental and powerful traditional prayers of the entire Church together in the same place? (I'm thinking of prayers such as the Our Father, the Hail Mary, the Creed, and the Glory Be.) If you thought of the Rosary, you are certainly correct, but in our next section, following Thomas's lead, I'd like to emphasize another special place where all these prayers can also be found as a part of the greatest prayer of all. So now we turn to the greatest of all prayers and to the rite of the greatest of all sacraments, the Holy Sacrifice of the Mass.[88]

Celebrating the Highest Sacrament of All

Mass attendance is of extreme importance because there we find Christ present in a more real, profound, and mysterious way than

---

[88] I should note that while the Hail Mary is not said as a part of the Mass, it is prayed by the priest and the congregation three times while kneeling as a part of a series of prayers that follow the end of the Low Mass of the Traditional Latin or Extraordinary Form. Also, the Glory Be, not to be confused with the Gloria, is not found in the Novus Ordo Mass, but it is in the Extraordinary Latin form.

He can be found anywhere else on earth. While we will delve into Thomas's marvelous insights on the sacrament of the Eucharist in particular in chapter 12, here we will take a whirlwind tour of Thomas's primer on the Mass in the six articles of the *Summa Theologica*, part III, question 83: "Of the Rite of This Sacrament." Thomas will make crystal clear why we should go to Mass, and not merely to the woods, every Sunday.

Before we begin, let's note that while this chapter's life lesson encourages "going to" Mass, there is much more to this life lesson than that! Perhaps you have heard of the need for "active participation" in the Mass, and you do indeed need to participate, but be aware that such participation is far more than simply a matter of standing, sitting, kneeling, reciting verbal responses, or cracking open the hymnal at the right times. Christ said that we are to love God with all that we are, with "all your heart, and with all your soul, and with all your mind" (Matt. 22:37), not just with our knees and our vocal chords! This means we should *lift up our hearts to the Lord*, as we are encouraged to during each Mass, that we should also engage our minds by paying attention and by studying to learn about the majesty and mystery of the Mass, and by participating not only with the presence and movements of our physical bodies, but with all the strength that our souls can muster.

Thomas has so much to offer here that I encourage every reader to dig in deep into his words. The six articles on the rite of the Mass take up fewer than fifteen pages in double column print, and even if you do not own a copy of the *Summa Theologica*, it is available free online.[89] I will merely provide a few general

---

[89] Indeed, here is a direct link to III, 83: http://www.newadvent.org/summa/4083.htm.

highlights and details of interest in hopes of whetting your appetites for a deeper appreciation of the Mass and the importance of this chapter's life lesson.

In the first article of III, 83, Thomas starts by highlighting an essential element of the Mass that many may not realize in our modern (and modernist) times — indeed, perhaps one reason these times are so turbulent. Far more than merely a gathering of the faithful for a special meal, the Mass is a holy *sacrifice* of Christ. Citing St. Augustine, we find: "Christ was sacrificed once in Himself, and yet He is sacrificed daily in the Sacrament." In the Mass, we employ the words and gestures Christ used in establishing this sacrament at the Last Supper, but "this sacrament is an image representing Christ's Passion, which is His true sacrifice." Further, "by this sacrament, we are made partakers of the fruit of our Lord's Passion," and, indeed, "as the celebration of this sacrament is an image representing Christ's Passion, so the altar is representative of the cross itself, upon which Christ was sacrificed." If we remember that an altar is so much more than any dinner table, we will be in a much better position to give it, and the sacrifice made upon it, the ultimate reverence it deserves.

In the second article, on the time for celebrating Mass, Thomas answers some rather intriguing objections, such as the idea that since the Mass is commemorative of Christ's Passion, why do we not celebrate it just once per year on Good Friday? Thomas provides many interesting insights in the course of his elaborate answer, and here's one that caught my eye, regarding why Catholic priests celebrate Mass every day. Thomas begins by citing Christ's words in Luke 11:3, "give us each day our daily bread," and finishes with this thought from St. Augustine: "If it be a daily bread, why do you take it once a year, as the Greeks have the custom in the east? Receive it daily that it may benefit you every day."[90]

Article 3 of III, 83 addresses "Whether This Sacrament Ought to Be Celebrated in a House and with Sacred Vessels," and it is amazingly rich in insights that should increase our reverence for every house of the Lord, for every piece of furniture, every decoration, and every utensil it houses. Thomas uses the word "house" for the church, following St. Paul in his First Letter to Timothy (3:15): "You may know how one ought to behave in the household of God, which is the church of the living God." He then goes on to explain why churches, altars, and sacred vessels are consecrated to their special service to God. The altar is consecrated for example, because "by the altar Christ Himself is signified, of Whom the Apostle says (Heb. 13:15); *Through Him we offer a sacrifice of praise to God.*"

As for the sacredness of every single part of a consecrated church, note that even "the beams of a dedicated church" ought not to be used for any purpose other than for use in another church or monastery, and "on no account are they to be discarded for the works of laity." Similar limitations are prescribed for "the altar covering, chair, candlesticks, and veil."[91] A simple take-

---

[90]   Of course, we are obligated to attend Mass weekly, but more frequent or even daily attendance, if possible, provides yet more spiritual benefits, since, as we saw when addressing III, 83, 1, in each Holy Sacrifice of the Mass, "we are made partakers of the fruit of our Lord's Passion." Every Mass bears spiritual fruits for those who choose to receive and enjoy them!

[91]   As I read Thomas's words, I recall seeing for many years the magnificent hanging lights and pews of the once beautiful demolished church of my childhood inside a local upscale shopping mall before it closed its doors. The new church had no need for

home message I suggest from this article would be to support, however you can, the construction and reverent use, care, or restoration of beautiful churches, altars, vessels, and vestments, to show reverence for all the things used to serve God in His own household. Seek out a new, more reverent church, if necessary.

In the fourth article, Thomas addresses "Whether the Words Spoken in This Sacrament Are Properly Formed," and this is the first of two articles in which Thomas goes through each major individual part of the rite of the Mass, one by one. Now, living in the thirteenth century, Thomas writes, of course, about the old, Latin Mass, but if you attend the new Mass, you will still see the relevance of most of his insights, showing how every part of the Mass prepares us for proper reception of and gratitude for the Eucharist.

Here is just one rather intriguing insight. One of nine objections notes that in the Consecration of this sacrament, words are used that are not attributed to Christ in the Gospel. For example, "we do not read in the Gospel, of Christ lifting up his eyes to heaven while consecrating this sacrament." Thomas replies in the words of Scripture, noting first that in John 21:25, we are told that Christ said and did many things which are not written down by the Evangelists, but some of these have been passed down through tradition, including Christ's lifting His eyes up to heaven at the Last Supper. Further, the Gospel does reveal that before raising Lazarus from the dead "Jesus lifted his eyes," and in His prayer for the disciples at the Last Supper, Jesus "had more reason to do so in instituting this sacrament, as being of greater import."

---

the lights, since they would be replaced by recessed pot lights, pretty much like the kind we have in our informal family room.

Article 5, on "Whether the Actions Performed in Celebrating This Sacrament Are Becoming," drills down in great detail into the elaborate, ritually prescribed gestures of the priest during the Mass. I found Thomas's twelve objections, compiled in the thirteenth century, particularly interesting since some are the same objections I have heard against the Latin Mass expressed by modernist thinkers of the twentieth and twenty-first centuries!

For example, regarding the fifty-two times the priest makes the Sign of the Cross in the Latin Mass, objection 3 holds "the ceremonies performed in the sacraments of the Church ought not to be repeated. Consequently it is not proper for the priest to repeat the sign of the cross many times over this sacrament." Thomas responds to this one objection with nine specific, paragraph-long responses, spelling out the fascinating reasons and depths of meaning behind each *allegedly* perfunctory, excessively repetitive Sign of the Cross. Thomas notes that the Sign of the Cross signifies Christ's Passion, which occurred in stages (think, for a familiar example, of the Stations of the Cross). Each series of signs of the cross represents a spiritual lesson from each stage. Allow me to highlight just a few:

> Fifthly, the outstretching of Christ's body, and the shedding of the blood, and the fruits of the Passion, are signified by the triple signification of the cross at the words, *as many as shall receive the body and blood, may be filled with every blessing*, etc.
>
> Sixthly, Christ's threefold prayer upon the cross is represented; one for His persecutors when he said, *Father, forgive them*; the second for deliverance from death, when He cried, *My God, My God, why hast Thou forsaken Me?*; the third referring to His entrance into glory, when He

said, *Father, into Thy hands I commend My spirit*; and in order to denote these there is a triple signing with the cross made at the words, *Thou dost sanctify, quicken, bless.*

Seventhly, the three hours during which He hung upon the cross, that is, from the sixth to the ninth hour, are represented; in signification of which we make once more a triple sign of the cross at the words, *through Him, and with Him, and in Him.*

I won't extend this chapter much further with a detailed analysis of the sixth article on possible "defects," or problems that might occur during Mass, but I guarantee it makes for some interesting reading. Indeed, if you ever wondered what would happen if a forgetful priest said the words of consecration twice; if, due to the cold, the host slips from the priest's hand into the chalice and he cannot break it as prescribed; or even indeed, if a spider or some other poisonous creature fell into the chalice after the Consecration, rest assured that Thomas has supplied the answers![92]

To sum things up for this chapter, if you take the time to learn more about the Mass, if you seek out the most reverent Mass you can find, prepare for it with prayer, and put on your Sunday best, your weekly "obligation" will become a most glorious and fruitful privilege as well.

At the beginning of the traditional Mass, the priest, acting in the person of Christ, echoes the words of King David: "*Introibo ad altare Dei*" (I will go in to the altar of God). The servers respond:

[92] I won't keep you in total suspense, at least in regard to the poisoned chalice. Thomas explains that the creature should be removed, the chalice cleaned, and new wine consecrated. (Makes sense to me!)

"*Ad Deum qui laetificat juventutem meam*" (To God, who giveth joy to my youth").[93] Never forget that, every Sunday, your time contemplating the sacrifice of God's altar can rejuvenate you and bring you a joy that those who are merely "spiritual but not religious" can never fully experience or understand.

LIFE LESSON 9 SUMMA

God Himself has called us to be religious, and not merely spiritual. He gave us the first three commandments so our worship would be centered solely on Him, binding us to Him, who gives us all that we have and are. We are called to battle spiritual sloth and ignorance and to grow in the knowledge and the practice of the interior and exterior acts of religion, as guided by faith, hope, and charity. We should pray every day to God in thanks for all that He has given us, and at least once a week, we must gather in a church and pray with the Church the greatest of all prayers: the Mass, the holy vehicle in which God Himself comes into our hearts and souls in the most intimate way, exceeding even His presence, essence, and power present in the woods and throughout creation.

[93] The priest and servers then pray the *Judica Me* (Judge me), based on Psalm 43 (42). See also Ps. 103 (102):5, regarding God "who satisfies you with good as long as you live so that your youth is renewed like the eagles."

Listen to That Angel
on Your Shoulder

Though we are lower than the angels,
they are eager to raise us up.

Question 10

How can people in the twenty-first
century believe in angels?

Thomas answers that …

"There must be some incorporeal creatures. For what is
principally intended by God in creatures is good, and this
consists in assimilation to God Himself. . . . Now God
produces the creature by his intellect and will. Hence,
the perfection of the universe requires that there should
be intellectual creatures. Now intelligence cannot be the
action of a body, nor of any corporeal faculty limited
to here and now. Hence the perfection of the universe
requires the existence of an incorporeal creature."

—*Summa Theologica* I, 50, 1

Where Can We Learn about Angels?

God sometimes works in delightfully surprising ways. Little did I
know as I knelt in prayer before a Latin Mass yesterday morning
and included a petition for guidance in starting this chapter, that
in just a few minutes our Gradual Prayer would read as follows
(in English translation, that is):

God has given His Angels charge over thee, to keep thee in all thy ways. In their hands they shall bear thee up, lest thou dash thy foot against a stone.[94]

Further, we would hear in the course of the Gospel reading that the Devil recited this very verse to Jesus as he tempted Him to throw Himself down from the pinnacle of the Temple. Jesus responded: "It is written again, Thou shalt not tempt the Lord thy God" (Matt. 4:7, citing Deut. 6:16). While Jesus did not call upon the angels in that instance, we do know that they came to Him when He needed them most; for example, during His agonizing night of prayer in the Garden of Gethsemane, "there appeared to him an angel from heaven, strengthening him" (Luke 22:43). Further, legions of angels were always on standby, should Jesus call them into action. When Jesus bade Peter to put away his sword after a great armed crowd came to arrest Him, He declared: "Do you think I cannot appeal to my Father, and he will at once send me more than twelve legions of angels?" (Matt. 26:53).[95]

As Catholics, we should not hesitate to believe in angels, on the authority of both Scripture and Tradition. Jesus knew them and spoke to us about them. Of course, we even know some of them by name, such as Gabriel, who announced to young Mary that she had been selected by God to bring Christ into the world and, as we have seen, gave us the first words of the

---

[94] Gradual prayer for the First Sunday in Lent, from Ps. 91 (90):11–12.

[95] This event is reported in all four Gospels, though only in John 18 is Peter identified as the sword wielder and Malchus as the servant, and only in Luke 22 is it reported that Jesus healed the servant's ear.

Hail Mary (Luke 1:28). Angels were not unknown to the Jewish people either. They figure prominently in many books of the Old Testament, such as Michael in the book of Daniel and Raphael in Tobit. We learn that angels have different ranks and duties; Gabriel, Michael, and Raphael, for example, are referred to as "archangels." St. Paul's letters and various passages in Scripture mention nine ranks or orders. St. Thomas arranged and described them as shown in a table in our appendix.

We have already mentioned one other extremely powerful and unfortunately *infamous* angel in our citation from St. Matthew's Gospel. That angel, *fallen* angel to be exact, is the Devil, also known as Satan, and originally as Lucifer (light bearer), who turned against God, fell from heaven, cajoled many angels to join him in his rebellion, and persuaded our first parents to bring sin into the world.

Angels appear time and time again in many books of the Old and the New Testaments, from Genesis through Revelation. Theologians have elaborated on the angels over the centuries in the most intriguing and remarkable ways, and none more elaborately or intriguingly than our Angelic Doctor.

What Are Angels, and Why Should We Care?

We've touched on the question of where we can learn about angels, their various orders and duties, and even *who* some of them are, but we shouldn't go further until we've addressed just *what* they are. St. Thomas was indeed a stickler about defining terms! This probably will not come as a surprise to you, but we'll also turn to Thomas to delve into that answer—to define those beings and show how they fit into the divine design. Of course, Thomas is the Angelic Doctor, and one reason is the "Treatise on the Angels" that appears in the *Summa Theologica*, part I, questions

50–64. Not nearly finished with them yet, Thomas examines them in more depth in the "Treatise on Divine Government" in I, 106–114. Never has there been a more exhaustive examination of just what angels are and why they are so important. So let us fly to the Angelic Doctor and open his sublime treatises to see what light he can shine for us on his mighty, mysterious, numinous namesakes.

We should begin by noting that our word "angel" derives from the Greek word *angelos*, "messenger." Indeed, when we see angels in Scripture, they are often shown in just that role, as when the archangel Gabriel delivered to the Blessed Virgin Mary the most important of all messages. Thomas confirms that angels do indeed act on earth, fulfilling missions for God, citing for example, Exodus 23:20: "Behold I send an angel before you, to guard you on the way and to bring you to the place which I have prepared" in I, 112, 1. He notes in the next article, however, referencing St. Gregory the Great and Dionysius,[96] that the higher ranks of angels do *not* perform exterior services outside of heaven.

Let's now look at a sample of what Thomas said about what angels really are and some of their most profound and fascinating characteristics. Please note that every one of Thomas's conclusions about angels is presented within the context of very elaborate, nuanced counterarguments and replies based on scriptural references and philosophical and theological principles aplenty. Here I will leave out the vast majority of the discursive reasoning and merely provide a whirlwind tour of his bottom-line statements. In a sense this is particularly fitting for the subject of angels, since Thomas tells us that, unlike humans, angels do

---

[96] Please recall our footnote at the start of chapter 3 on the identity of Dionysius.

not require chains of reasoning to lead them to truth, but they acquire truths all at once and instantly, "as an object and its image are seen simultaneously in a mirror" (I, 58, 3). Of course, for those who would care to examine the reasoning behind St. Thomas's conclusions, I'll provide citations to direct you to the relevant questions and articles in the great *Summa* itself. So, without further adieu—up, up, and away we go to the angels!

- *Angels are incorporeal.* They do not have bodies. The perfection of the universe requires purely spiritual, intellectual creatures, which more perfectly reflect their Creator (I, 50, 1).[97]
- *Angels exist in great number.* Indeed, "it is reasonable to conclude that the immaterial substances as it were incomparably exceed material substances as to multitude" (I, 50, 3).[98]

---

[97] Thomas uses natural reason and divine revelation to examine the existence and the nature of angels, creatures who reflect the Creator in their immaterial, bodiless, spiritual nature. Inanimate objects, such as rocks, have matter, but no soul. Plants have material bodies and souls, but lack the ability to sense and perceive the world. Animals have bodies and souls too, along with the ability to know particular things. Humans have bodies and souls, but our souls have *spiritual, intellectual* capacities that allow us to grasp universal principles, to understand things, and to seek what we deem good through the power of free will. Our spiritual intellects and wills must operate, though, on the data that comes from our bodily senses. Angels complete the hierarchy of created beings, possessing yet higher intelligence and will, without any dependence on a material body.

[98] Thomas's scriptural reference here is the heavenly mystical vision around the throne in Daniel 7:10: "A thousand thousands served him, and ten thousand times ten thousand stood before him."

• *Angels do not die.* As purely spiritual beings, they contain no matter that can decompose. They could only lapse into nothingness, as would all created bodily and spiritual things, if God should no longer sustain them in being (I, 50, 5).

• *Angels can assume bodies* in fulfillment of God's missions on earth. Their bodies are more than imaginary visions of the person they visit, since Scripture records incidents when angels are seen commonly by all, "just as the angels who appeared to Abraham were seen by him and his whole family, by Lot, and by the citizens of Sodom; in like manner the angel who appeared to Tobias was seen by all present" (I, 51, 2).

• *Angels, though spiritual, can be in a place.* Though angels have no bodies or measurable quantity, Thomas concluded that they are in only one place at a time, not in the sense that they are *contained by it*, but in the sense of somehow *containing it* as the soul is in the body by containing it, not by being contained by it (I, 52, 2).

• *Angels can, however, apply their power to only one place at a time* (I, 52, 3).

• *Angels in assumed bodies can move from place to place, passing through successive locations* (I, 53, 1).

• *Angels as pure spirit can pass from one place to another without going through the points in between.* "Now, the actual passing from one extreme to the other, without going through the mid-space is quite in keeping with an angel's nature; but not with that of a body" (I, 53, 2).

• *Angels derive their knowledge of creatures in the material world not through bodily senses, as we do,* but "there are images of creatures in the angel's mind, not, indeed, derived from creatures, but from God, Who is the cause of creatures, and in Whom the likeness of creatures first exist" (I, 55, 2).

* *Angels of higher orders understand more deeply than angels of lower orders* because they have a more universal knowledge, closer, though still infinitely removed from that of God who knows everything through one thing, the divine essence (I, 55, 3).[99]
* *Angels know material things and individuals, but do not, however, know the future, our secret thoughts, or fully grasp the mysteries of God's grace* (I, 57, 1–5).
* *Angels can understand many things at the same time.* "Consequently, by such knowledge as the angels have of things through the Word, they know all things under one intelligible species, which is the Divine essence. Therefore, as regards such knowledge, they know all things at once" (I, 58, 3).[100]
* *Angels, like us, have free will and natural love for themselves* (I, 59 and 60).

[99] Thomas draws an earthly parallel here: "An example of this can in some measure be observed in ourselves. For some people there are who cannot grasp an intelligible truth, unless it be explained to them in every part and detail; this comes of their weakness of intellect; while there are others of stronger intellect, who can grasp many things from few" (I, 55, 3). (I submit that the extent of St. Thomas's intellectual grasp is indeed another reason he merits the title Angelic Doctor.)

[100] Bear in mind that Thomas is saying that angels know all that they know at once, and not that like God, they know everything there is to know at once. We saw above, for example, that they do not know things such as the future or our innermost thoughts.

• *Angels reside in heaven and were created by God at the same time he created the material world.* Thomas tells us, citing Strabus,[101] that when the first words of the Bible tell us, "In the beginning God created the heavens and the earth" (Gen. 1:1), "By heaven he does not mean the visible firmament, but the empyrean, that is the fiery or intellectual firmament, which is not so styled from its heat, but from its splendor; and which was filled with angels directly it was made" (I, 61, 4).

I'll stop here with the angelic highlights, since we have so much more celestial ground to cover related to this chapter's life lesson, on remembering to call on the angels. I hope you have a taste now for what angels are, as Thomas has helped us penetrate some of their most principal principles. We'll zoom in directly on why we should care about angels in the very next section, on pulverizing the sins that can hold us back from acting on this life lesson, and become, in a sense, a little more angelic.

Pulverizing That Devil Sitting on Your Shoulder

We've all seen the cartoons showing a little devil on a person's shoulder, whispering into one ear, while a little angel sits on his other shoulder, whispering opposing advice into the other ear. Indeed, retentive readers will recall that the title of this chapter is "Listen to That Angel on Your Shoulder!" I imagine that only readers as old as or (heaven forbid) older than I am will remember from the 1970s the comedian Flip Wilson's character "Geraldine," whose most famous line was, "The Devil made me do it!" In fact, I just watched online on old skit in which, defending her actions before her husband, she blames the devil for making her

---

[101] Walafrid Strabo (ca. 808–849), Benedictine monk and theologian.

buy three dresses in the same week and for crashing her car into a church. She describes scenarios in which the devil not only tempts, cajoles, and tries to persuade her but grabs her steering wheel and even pulls a gun on her—to compel her to buy that third dress![102] Such cartoons and skits are crafted in fun, with a humorous intent, but they also raise a serious question. Can the devil or his subordinate demons really *make us* do it? Thankfully, St. Thomas has provided a clear answer.

St. Thomas says "the devil can nowise compel man to sin" (I-II, 80, 3). But we must still, so to speak, give the devil his due; in this case, meaning due acknowledgment of what he *can do* in regard to moving or *tempting us* to sin. St. Thomas notes that the devil does not have power over our free will. Scripture tells us, for example: "Resist the devil and he will flee from you" (James 4:7). The devil can tempt us by stirring our sensitive appetites and imaginations, feeding us with impulses and images that lure us toward sin, but God has not allowed him dominion over our intellectual souls. As Augustine has noted, "nothing else than his own will makes man's mind the slave of his desire" (cited by St. Thomas in I-II, 80, 1). How important, then, to train ourselves in virtue and to render ourselves open to God's grace, so that we may "just say no" to the devil!

Angelic Goads to Virtue

If we are to practice the virtues that good angels would bid us to do, we must begin with the virtue of *faith*, believing in God and all that He has revealed, including the reality and the power of

---

[102] When her husband asks Geraldine why she didn't slam on the brake when the devil grabbed the steering wheel, she replies she was busy trying to kick him!

angels. This includes a basic awareness of not only the heavenly angels, but also the demons of hell, and where both of them came from.

In I, 63, 4, Thomas asks "Whether Any of the Demons Are Naturally Wicked." The key word here is "naturally," and the answer, in one word, is "No!" Everything God has created is good in the very fact that it has being. "It is written (Gen. 1:31): *God saw all the things that He made, and they were very good.* But among them were the demons. Therefore the demons were at some time good" (I, 64, 5). And speaking of very good, the devil himself, by the nature God gave him, was the very highest of the angels. God gave the angels intellects and wills, and those that became evil did so through their own power of choice. And what was the devil's evil choice? "It is said, in the person of the devil (Isa. 14:13–14), *I will ascend into heaven. . . . I will be like the Most High*" (I, 63, 3).

Thomas elaborates that the devil's sin of pride consisted of seeking to exist, not as the glorious creature God made him, but as God Himself. He sought to attain his own last end of beatitude, not in cooperation with God's grace, but entirely according to his own power, which belongs to God alone and not to even the highest of creatures. He sought as well to be like God in dominion over others. He used his free will to reject God and thereby fell from God's grace and embraced evil, irrevocably rejecting the lofty degree of perfection that was possible to him.

We learn from Revelation 12:4 that "the dragon *drew* with him *the third part of the stars of heaven.*" The devil did not *cause* a third of the angels to sin and reject God, but he *induced* and exhorted them to make that irrevocable choice of their own free will. They proudly chose him as their prince to lead them to the beatitude they, too, would obtain without the aid of God.

It is the same kind of power that Satan exercised on a third of the angels that he and his demonic minions try to exercise upon our souls, so we need to be aware of them and their tactics.[103] The presence and action of Satan and his demons is expressed explicitly in Scripture time and again, and throughout the history of the Church. Indeed, in regard to the seven deadly sins, demons were recognized to play a role sometimes in inducing us into such sins. *Acedia*, or *sloth*, which we've met a few times already in these pages, was called "the noonday devil" by the ancient Desert Fathers, drawing from Psalm 91:6: "the destruction that wastes at noonday." St. John Climacus (579–649), for example, wrote that the desert monk afflicted by the "noonday" demon of *acedia* will become bored by his prayers, will feel fatigue and weakness, will feel like leaning while standing and like sitting while leaning. It will lead to distractions. At the slightest noise, the hermit will look out his window. Further, some theologians even provided names for the demons who encouraged each of the deadly sins.

While we must be aware of fallen angels and their powers to tempt us, we must remember Thomas's lesson that they cannot *compel* us to sin, and the ultimate virtue, that crucial addition to *faith*, that will allow us to resist them, is again that highest virtue, *charity*. Recall the words of St. James: "Even the demons believe — and shudder" (James 2:19). They believe in God, of course, but their *faith* is useless and barren because it lacks *charity*, which produces not sin but good works.

Not only should we recognize our power to resist fallen angels, but, just as importantly, we should recognize that good angels are

---

[103] Readers are directed to C. S. Lewis's *Screwtape Letters* for a masterful depiction of many of their tactics in modern times.

indeed there on our shoulders, prodding us toward charity and all manner of virtues, and we should train ourselves to listen to them. Thomas has written a full eight articles on "Of the Guardianship of the Good Angels" (I, 113), and it would behoove us right now to take a peek at some of the most fascinating and useful highlights:

- *Angels guard human beings.* "For he will give his angels charge of you to guard you in all your ways" (I, 133, 1, citing Ps. 91 [90]:11).
- *"Each man has an angel guardian appointed to him.* This rests upon the fact that the guardianship of angels belongs to the execution of Divine providence concerning men" (I, 133, 2).
- *Angels of the lowest order guard individual human beings,* while "guardianship of the human race belongs to the order of *Principalities,* or perhaps to the *Archangels,* whom we call the angel princes. Hence Michael, whom we call an archangel, is also styled *one of the princes"* (I, 133, 3, citing Dan. 10:13).
- *Every person has a guardian angel as long as he lives on earth.* "When he arrives at the end of life he no longer has a guardian angel; but in the kingdom he will have an angel to reign with him, in hell a demon to punish him" (I, 133, 4).
- *An angel is appointed to guard us at the time of birth* (citing St. Jerome). And now behold this beautiful statement from the Angelic Doctor on angels and the dignity of the *unborn:* "As long as the child is in the mother's womb, it is not entirely separate, but by reason of a certain intimate tie, is still part of her: just as the fruit while hanging on the tree is part of the tree. And therefore it can be said

with some degree of probability, that the angel who guards the mother guards the child while in the womb. But at its birth, when it becomes separate from the mother, an angel guardian is appointed to it; as Jerome, above quoted, says" (I, 133, 5).

Angelic Prayer

What a difference it should make in our daily lives on earth to think there is an angel watching over every one of us! Yet, how often do we ever reflect on this (except perhaps that one day every year before Christmas, when we watch George Bailey and his guardian angel, Clarence, in *It's a Wonderful Life*)? One way to remind ourselves of the angels' presence, and to avail ourselves of their aid, is to think of their presence in some of our most beloved prayers. In the Our Father, when we acknowledge that God is in heaven and His will is done there, we can recall that in heaven God dwells with the great myriad of angels, who exist to praise Him and do His will, which includes how He wills them to help us. The Hail Mary should also remind us of the beautiful and mysterious reality of angels, since its opening salute quotes the archangel Gabriel. Of course, the Angelus starts with the words "The angel of the Lord declared unto Mary." Every mention of heaven in the Creed should also remind us of angels.

Perhaps even more importantly, we should remember to pray for the intercession of our own guardian angels, and to pray prayers dedicated to particular angels, including the powerful prayer Pope Leo XIII added to the end of the Low Mass in 1886—another time when the Church was threatened by the growing darkness of secularism and early modernistic ideas—the Prayer to St. Michael the Archangel:

St. Michael the Archangel,
defend us in battle.
Be our defense against the wickedness
  and snares of the devil.
May God rebuke him, we humbly pray,
and do thou,
O Prince of the heavenly hosts,
by the power of God,
thrust into hell Satan,
and all the evil spirits,
who prowl about the world
seeking the ruin of souls. Amen.

In 1994, Pope John Paul II wrote: "Although this prayer is no longer recited at the end of Mass, I ask everyone not to forget it and to recite it to obtain help in the battle against the forces of darkness and against the spirit of this world."[104] This prayer does remain at the end of Traditional Low Masses, and several years ago, the bishop of my diocese, and the bishops of several others, have reinstated it at the end of the Novus Ordo as well. *St. Michael the Archangel, defend us in these turbulent times!*

Angels at the Altar of the Highest Sacrament

We started this chapter with a reference to the angels in the Mass of the First Sunday in Lent. We should be well aware, however, that we are surrounded by angels, who join in our prayers, throughout *every* Holy Sacrifice of the Mass. Many saints and Church Doctors, including St. Augustine, St. John Chrysostom, and Pope St. Gregory the Great, have written of the angels'

[104] John Paul II, *Regina Caeli*, April 24, 1994.

presence at Mass, and some, including St. Bridget of Sweden, Blessed Henry Suso, and St. Padre Pio, have even experienced their mystical presence at Mass.

Though most of us have probably not been blessed with such an angelic mystical vision, if you are blessed to have a church with a high altar, the odds are pretty good that you see at least *statues* of angels there. The practice goes very, very far back. When Bezalel of the tribe of Judah, filled with the Spirit of God and blessed with the gift of craftsmanship, built the Ark of the Covenant before the time of Christ, he adorned it with two angels of gold. "The cherubim spread out their wings above, overshadowing the mercy seat with their wings, with their fiery faces one to another" (Exod. 37:9).

Indeed, my earliest memories of Mass include two elegant angels flanking Christ upon a prominent crucifix. Lest we think such depictions are quaint and truly childish distractions, outgrown by the maturity of our current "modern man," let's recall again some wise words from St. Thomas: "spiritual impressions easily slip from the mind, unless they be tied as it were to some corporeal image, because human knowledge has a greater hold on sensible objects" (II-II, 49, 1).

As for the Holy Sacrifice of the Mass itself, the angels play most significant roles in both forms of the Mass. Here are but a few examples:

- The *Confiteor* of the Latin Mass prays for the intercession of blessed Michael the Archangel, while the corresponding *Penitential Rite* of the Novus Ordo asks for the prayers of all the angels.
- The *Gloria* builds upon the words of the angel who appeared to announce Christ's birth to the shepherds and who was suddenly surrounded by a multitude of angels

praising God and saying: "Glory to God in the highest, and on earth peace to people of good will" (see Luke 2:14).

- When in the *Sanctus* or the *Preface Acclamation* the priest prays, "Sanctus, Sanctus, Sanctus" or "Holy, Holy, Holy," he echoes the seraphim surrounding God's heavenly throne (Isa. 6:3; Rev. 4:8).

Speaking of angels, sacraments, and the Angelic Doctor, we should note as well that the Blessed Sacrament has been referred to as "the bread of angels," echoing the description of the manna from heaven (Ps. 78 [77]:25), and if you have ever heard Pavarotti, Bocelli, or any other great singer or choir sing "Panis Angelicus" (Bread of the Angels), the title and the lyrics come from the hymn "Sacris Solemnis Juncta Sint Gaudia" (Let Joys Be Joined to Solemn Feasts), first written for the then-new solemn and joyous feast of Corpus Christi (The Body of Christ) by none other than our own Angelic Doctor, St. Thomas Aquinas. It would appear that he never forgot the angel on his shoulder or the God-made-man they adore in body and spirit.

LIFE LESSON 10 SUMMA

God has crafted us higher than the animals and lower than the angels in raw perfection of being, and yet He assigned angels to attend not only to His Son as the Incarnate God-man, but also to every one of us. We should take time to learn about, think about, pray to, and listen to the guardian angels "on our shoulders" and the angels all around us, especially at Mass, so that we might grow in faith, and, like the angels, better serve God in charity. We should be aware of the capacity of fallen angels to tempt us to all manner of sins and of the fact that God has not allowed them power to overcome our free will to resist temptation and send them fleeing. Many of the most beautiful prayers and hymns on earth were inspired by, spoken by, or refer to God's holy angels. May we pray that the angels might help us become more angel-like on earth so that we may one day pray, "Holy! Holy! Holy!" with them around God's throne in heaven.

Be a Saint

We must learn about, pray to, and imitate the saints
so that we may become saints too.

Question 11

The Bible tells us Jesus is the one Mediator. Do we also need saints?

Thomas answers ...

"Do not fail to imitate the lives of saintly and noble men."

—*Letter to Brother John on How to Study*

Born (and Reborn) for Sainthood

When the young friar Brother John wrote to St. Thomas for advice on how to study effectively and train one's mind to grasp the truth, among the simple maxims Thomas gave him was the one that is shown above. God gave every human being, and only human beings of all living species on earth, intellects through which we can obtain universal truths and wills through which we can apply moral truths in the daily acts of our lives. So, Brother John's question on how to improve his intellectual powers was indeed a good one. Of course, the ultimate truth that we seek, with a capital *T*, is Truth Himself, or God, and the ultimate good we seek with a capital G is also God Himself, as Thomas made clear to us in chapter 1, when we examined our first and foundational life lesson.

12 Life Lessons from St. Thomas Aquinas

Now, Thomas knew well that *to achieve that ultimate goal, we are all, in fact, called to become saints.* "Sanctity" means "holiness," and we have been explicitly told regarding the gate of heaven that "nothing unclean shall enter it" (Rev. 21:27). Jesus made clear in His famous mountain sermon: "You, therefore, must be perfect, as your heavenly Father is perfect" (Matt. 5:48). We must attain a pure holiness to see God, whether we attain a high state of holiness by our last days on earth, or through purging of venial sins in purgatory.

The men and women officially declared saints by the Church have all passed with highest honors our first life lesson, having entered the gate of heaven, through their heroic cooperation with the bountiful graces of God. They did not pull themselves to heaven by their own bootstraps. They knew that "unless one is born anew, he cannot see the kingdom of God," and further, "unless one is born of water and the Spirit, he cannot enter the kingdom of God" (John 3:3, 5). Being baptized into God's Church and filled with God's graces, the saints so conformed their intellects and wills to the truth and the goodness of God that they not only won the prize of heaven but also stand ready, willing, and able to help *us* cross that celestial finish line and join them.

Not every saint was a scholar, but every one of them gave his or her all to God in mind, body, and soul — and we would do well to imitate them. When the twentieth-century social-learning-theory psychologists, most prominently Albert Bandura, scientifically verified the power of social learning theory (also known as learning through imitation or "modeling"), especially through research on children, they were quantifying more precisely what has long been commonsense wisdom. We have all heard and grasped the implications of the saying "Do what I say, not what I do!" — not to mention "Monkey see, monkey do!"

Many can probably think of examples of such monkey business they have seen in action, and some of you might even admit to having been the monkey, at least once![105]

The Church has long known of this powerful principle too. Come to think of it, we started this book with one bit of advice that even predates the Church, coming from the Old Testament: "He who walks with wise men becomes wise" (Prov.13:20). The particular wise man I had in mind was St. Thomas Aquinas, and that wise man has advised us to walk with the saints, never failing to imitate them. Of course, we cannot imitate what we do not know, so if we are to live out this life lesson we must strive to make time to learn about the saints. Indeed, one of the great blessings of the Catholic Faith is that we are blessed with a vast multitude of saints who stand ready for our imitation. Countless books have been written about their saintly lives, and many saints have left us with the most remarkable books of their own.

Few practiced this imitation of the saints more eagerly and assiduously than St. Thomas. Listen to this papal testimony regarding Thomas's love for the wisdom of the saintly theological teachers who came before him, and how it raised him to unparalleled heights:

[105] When I would expand on the power of imitation to my developmental-psychology students, I described the first time I saw my toddler son get up on his tiptoes and carefully raise one leg high in the air to turn off the television set with his toes (an admirable, monkey-like feat of dexterity for a child of his age). I realized though, as soon as I saw him do it, that *I* was the big monkey he imitated, having many a night, before his eyes, carried his sleeping older brother to bed, and with hands occupied, turned off the TV with my toe, a feat requiring far less dexterity!

12 Life Lessons from St. Thomas Aquinas

Now far above all other Scholastic Doctors towers Thomas Aquinas, their master and prince. Cajetan says truly of him: "So great was his veneration for the ancient and sacred Doctors that he may be said to have gained a perfect understanding of them all." Thomas gathered their doctrines like the scattered limbs of a body, and moulded them into a whole. He arranged them in so wonderful an order, and increased them with such great additions, that rightly and deservedly he is reckoned a singular safeguard and glory of the Catholic Church.[106]

To read the *Summa Theologica* and many other of Thomas's great works, is to come across hundreds, no, *many thousands*, of citations from hundreds of great saints and dozens of Church Fathers and Church Doctors of the Eastern and Western Church. Indeed, thanks to modern computerized word-searching technology, one modern author notes that among various theologians cited in the *Summa Theologica*, St. Augustine takes home the gold, so to speak, with an astounding 3,156 references, St. Gregory the Great takes home the silver at 761, and the bronze goes to Dionysius at 607.[107] It's no wonder we've already come across all three of them many times within *these* pages! Thomas's

---

[106] Pope Leo XIII, Encyclical Letter *Aeterni Patris, On the Restoration of Christian Philosophy According to the Mind of St. Thomas Aquinas, The Angelic Doctor* (August 4, 1879). (I aver that one of the main reasons these are such turbulent times is that too few modern thinkers have shown similar veneration and understanding for the doctrines of the Angelic Doctor, rendering the Church less safe for those within it and less glorious in the eyes of the world.)

[107] Stephen Beale, "Which Church Fathers Most Influenced St. Thomas Aquinas?" *National Catholic Register*, February 8, 2018.

Catena Aurea (Golden Chain) on the Gospels weaves together verse-by-verse commentary from several dozen Latin and Greek Church Fathers.

Thomas was interested in the saints not only as guides to his philosophical and theological research, teaching, and writing, but as guides to his own spiritual life in pursuit of holiness. His friend Brother Reginald reports, for example, that Thomas always carried on his person relics of the early martyr St. Agnes of Rome, and once, when Reginald fell sick during one of their journeys, Thomas applied her relics to Reginald and prayed for her intercession. Reginald was cured, and Thomas began an annual feast for his students on St. Agnes's feast day.[108]

Though our primary focus in this life lesson is on saints, I should not neglect to mention that Thomas advised Brother John to imitate the lives not only of saintly people but of "noble" people too. Thomas lived out this lesson exceedingly well. He also eagerly sought out the pearls and nuggets of truth and wisdom in the writings of those he knew did not possess the fullness of truth of the Catholic Church, thinkers such as the pagans Aristotle, Plato, Cicero, Seneca, and others, the Jewish Maimonides, and

---

http://www.ncregister.com/blog/sbeale/which-church-fathers-most-influenced-st.-thomas-aquinas

[108] St. Agnes of Rome (291–304) is often depicted with a lamb since *agnus* means "lamb" in Latin. She was a virgin martyr, is one of seven women commemorated by name in the Traditional Canon of the Mass, and happens to be the namesake of my childhood church and grade school. For an insightful article on St. Thomas and St. Agnes, see Brother Joseph Martin Hagan, O.P., "The Lamb and the Dumb Ox," *Dominicana,* January 21 (her feast day), 2016. https://www.dominicanajournal.org/the-lamb-and-the-dumb-ox/.

the Arabs Averroes and Avicenna.[109] Thomas cherished truths wherever they may be found, and indeed, this is a hallmark of the Catholic Church herself. Revelation fears no truths of reason, for there is only one truth. While some in his day complained that he was watering down the wine of faith with the water of human wisdom, Thomas replied that "those who use philosophical doctrine in sacred Scripture in such a way as to subject them to the service of the faith, do not mix water with wine, but change water into wine."[110]

Sainthood Is for Sinners

The only man who lived completely without sin was the God-man, God Incarnate, Jesus Christ. The only woman who lived completely without sin, was, through the power and grace of God, the Mother of God, the Blessed Virgin Mary. Note well that this means that *every other human saint was, like us, a sinner*. Every other saint in the history of the Church on earth has had, like us, to strive to pulverize sin as he or she ascended the spiritual ladder toward God.

Now, some saints were indeed rather saintly, even from a tender age. We do not know of any truly serious sins in the life of our own Angelic Doctor, for example. We are told that he was always asking about God from about the time he learned

---

[109] Aristotle clearly took home the gold in terms of numbers of citations. Not only did Thomas write line-by-line commentaries on several of Aristotle's books, Aristotle, or "the Philosopher" is cited 2,095 times in the *Summa Theologica* (per Beale's previously cited article)!

[110] See section 2.3, ad. 5 in St. Thomas Aquinas, *Commentary on Boethius' On the Trinity*, St. Isidore Forum, https://isidore.co/aquinas/english/BoethiusDeTr.htm#L22.

how to talk. By the age of five, he was under the tutelage of the Benedictines at Monte Cassino. By the age of nineteen, he had joined the Dominican Order of Preachers. He was soon after kidnapped by his siblings in an attempt to get him to leave the order. When they sent a prostitute into his room, he chased her away with a blazing firebrand. Two angels visited him in his sleep and strengthened him in chastity that did not fail for the rest of his life. Indeed, the priest who heard Thomas's last confession before his death at age forty-nine said that Thomas's confessed sins were like those of an innocent child. Recall, too, Thomas's devotion to the virgin St. Agnes, who, at the tender age of thirteen had the holy fortitude to accept the martyr's crown.

Still, many, and perhaps most, of the saints of the Church were not nearly so angelic in their lives before they met Christ. The beloved St. Mary Magdalene who stood at the foot of the Cross and was the first to witness Christ's Resurrection, had earlier been healed of seven demons (Mark 16:9; Luke 8:2). Christ ministered to sinners, to prostitutes and sinful tax collectors, showing how they, through Him, could conquer sin, and countless sinners have done so since his Death and Resurrection. St. Mary of Egypt (344–421), for example, had been a prostitute for seventeen years before she converted to Christ and went on to become a desert hermit and a patron saint for persons undergoing sexual temptations. Her contemporary, the great St. Augustine of Hippo (354–430), had succumbed to sexual temptations of his own as a young man, having an illegitimate son with a concubine. Indeed, we find in his *Confessions* that at one time in his youth he had famously uttered in prayer: "Grant me chastity and continence, but not yet."

Many men and women have become great saints despite worse sins than sins of lust. Among the greatest of them all, St. Paul, before his dramatic conversion to Christ on the road to Damascus, was known as Saul, among the greatest persecutors of the early Christians, a man who was present at the stoning of St. Stephen, "consenting to his death" (Acts 8:1).

St. Patrick of Ireland (ca. 385–461), was born in Britain and carried to Ireland by Irish pirates before the age of sixteen. Though he was the son of a deacon, he reported that he did not take his Faith seriously until the almost seven years of his captivity, during which he learned to pray to God one hundred times per day and as many times at night. He, too, was subject to sin as a young man. As a middle-aged man and a bishop he wrote his own remarkable *Confession*, in which he lamented that a friend had reported him to Church authorities for a sin he confessed to him that he had committed as a youth before he converted to Christ, which lasted less than an hour, and was never repeated.[111]

Read almost any life of almost any saint, and you will see that he or she did indeed grapple with sin, oftentimes even after conversion to Christ, though they all made great strides in conquering sin through the graces of the Holy Spirit and the sacraments Christ gave us. We can follow their examples and do likewise.

Sins we must avoid regarding the saints and saintliness include the grave sin of *presumption*, whereby we presume either by overconfidence in our own ability to earn salvation without God's help in attaining sanctity, or by presuming of God that He will grant us our salvation without effort to attain sanctity on our part, and it's opposite extreme of *despair*, whereby we completely

---

[111] We do not know the nature of that sin of his adolescence.

abandon our hope that God can help us become saintly and enjoy eternal bliss with Him in heaven.[112]

Heroically Virtuous Saints Think, Do, and Love

Thomas examines differences in the types of lives that Christian saints may be called to live. These primary callings are to the *contemplative* life, which focuses on the inward contemplation of truth, and the *active* life, which focuses on external actions and affairs in the world. "Accordingly, since certain men are especially intent on the contemplation of truth, while others are especially intent on external actions, it follows that man's life is fittingly divided into active and contemplative" (II-II, 179, 1).

These categories derive from the very nature of the human intellectual soul. "The life of plants consists of nourishment and generation; the life of animals of sensation and movement; and the life of men in their understanding and acting according to reason" (II-II, 179, 1). God gave us the capacities to *know* truth and to *act* for good. We see this in the two main functions of our reasoning powers, by the workings of the *speculative* intellect, which contemplates truths and is perfected by the intellectual virtues of understanding, science, and reason; and by the workings of the *practical* intellect, which gets things done and is perfected by the virtues of art and prudence.

Thomas draws heavily on the writings of St. Gregory the Great in his comparisons and contrasts of the contemplative and active lives.[113] In using an example from the Old Testament,

---

[112] Despair and presumption have been traditionally listed among the sins against the Holy Spirit. They are addressed in sections on the virtue of hope in CCC 2091 and 2092.

[113] Gregory was a fascinating example of a man who by inclination was a contemplative hermit, and yet who was called by

Gregory wrote that Jacob's wife Leah, who was "blear-eyed" (see Gen. 29:17), but fruitful "signifies the active life; which being occupied with work, sees less, and yet since it urges one's neighbor both by word and example to its imitation begets a number of offspring of good deeds" (II-II, 182, 1, citing Gregory's *Homily on Ezekiel*). Gregory notes further that, "*the contemplative life gives beauty to the soul*, wherefore it is signified by Rachel, of *whom* it is said (Gen. 29:17) that she was *of a beautiful countenance.*"

The most famous biblical example is that of Martha, representing the active life, and her sister, Mary, the contemplative. Jesus declared, "Martha, Martha, you are anxious and troubled about many things; one thing is needful. Mary has chosen the good portion, which shall not be taken away from her" (Luke 10:41–42). Here we see Christ's acknowledgement of the value of contemplation. Gregory would say: "Great are the merits of the active life, but greater still those of the contemplative" (II-II, 182, 2). Thomas would note as well that the contemplative part will not be taken away since our eternal bliss will consist in the Beatific Vision of God.

The bottom-line Thomistic life lesson here is that God has called us all, like the saints, to contemplate the truth *and* to do

---

God to the busy office of the papacy. So well did he pursue that active life that he became one of a handful of popes to be called "the Great," and yet he lamented the loss of his contemplative bliss on heavenly things. "But now," he wrote while pope, "by reason of my pastoral charge, my poor soul is enforced to endure the burden of secular men's business, and after so sweet a kind of rest." Edmund G. Gardner, ed., *The Dialogues of St. Gregory the Great* (Merchantville, N.J.: Evolution Publishing, 2010), 4.

the good. At the risk of oversimplification, I like to think of these tasks in plain and simple terms as *thinking* and *doing*. We are all called to think and do, though some saints are so accomplished and well known in one area or the other that we might classify them as *thinkers* or *doers*, thinkers including the great theologians such as our own Thomas, as well as famous mystics such as Sts. John of the Cross and Teresa of Avila, and doers, including many saints who founded orders, such as Sts. Benedict and Ignatius of Loyola.

The nineteenth-century French Catholic psychologist Henri Joly has noted another interesting distinction we can make among the saints. "Throughout the history of the Church, there would seem to have been two distinct classes of saints. There are saints who personify active love and tenderness and there are saints who personify energetic action and the spirit of eager propagandism."[114] Those energetic evangelistic souls personify our *doers*, while those known best for their active love and tenderness could well be described as *lovers*. This is why I find it handy and profitable to think of saints in the threefold scheme of *thinkers*, *doers*, and *lovers*.[115] While all saints do all three, some are known best for one of those activities.

When Joly expanded on his two classes of saints, examples he gave included St. Dominic among what we are calling the doers, and St. Francis of Assisi as an exemplar lover. I first wrote about these classes of saints when writing about three Irish saints. St.

---

[114] Henri Joly, *The Psychology of the Saints* (Fort Collins, CO: Roman Catholic Books, n.d.), 50.

[115] Note, too, that while the intellectual virtues are so crucial to thinkers, and the moral virtues to doers, the theological virtues of faith, hope, and, foremost, loving charity ring out most clearly in our lovers.

Kevin of Glendalough, a hermit priest, abbot, and author, was the exemplar thinker; St. Patrick, the man from across the Irish sea who converted an entire nation, was the exemplar doer; and St. Brigid of Kildare, known most for intimate, interpersonal acts of hospitality, mercy, and kindness to the sick, to the poor, and even often to animals, was the exemplar lover.

As we examine saints from all times and all lands we can come up with all kinds of parallels. Let's take France for one more example. The greatest of all saintly *thinkers* was born in Italy but did his greatest work as a writer and professor at the University of Paris. I refer, of course, to our own St. Thomas. Next, there are certainly few saintly *doers* who have outdone the accomplishments of a young French girl. Indeed, the great American humorist Mark Twain, sometimes critical of religion in his works, was so enamored with her that he wrote an acclaimed historical novel all about her — the "her" being "the Maid of Orleans," St. Joan of Arc. And as for French saints known for *loving*, who can forget the lessons of the young lady who taught us all how to glorify God by throwing Him the flowers of the small, loving acts we perform every day. I refer, of course to "the Little Flower," St. Thérèse of Lisieux.

The saints personify for us virtue in action. Indeed, in the words of Pope Benedict XIV: "For the canonization of a servant of God, it is sufficient that there be proof that he has practiced those virtues which occasion demanded, in an eminent and heroic degree, according to his condition in life, rank and circumstances."[116] To imitate the saints is to grow in all manner of virtues, indeed, the good Lord willing, "in an eminent and

---

[116] Benedict XIV, *On the Beatification and Canonization of Saints* 3:21 (as cited in Joly, *The Psychology of the Saints*, 25).

heroic degree." *Every* saint, *in his or her own way*, lived out *all* of our life lessons, *and is ready to help show us how.* Time spent learning about the saints is time well spent, indeed.

Praying Like (and to) the Saints

Through the wonderful graces of God, we can also do much more than merely *learn about* the saints as we might learn about notable historical figures. We can also *form relationships with them* while on our way to joining them in heaven. We can show them honor by granting them the *dulia* that justice requires, as we learned in chapter 4. We can and should also pray to them to intercede with God for us. Christ is the only direct Mediator between man and God (1 Tim. 2:5), being both man and God, but He also established the Church, which gives us the saints who intercede for us in heaven. As St. John has told us, before the throne of God are "golden bowls full of incense, which are the prayers of the saints" (Rev. 5:8). The saints in heaven experience the Beatific Vision of God. They need not petition God for anything for themselves. Their sweet-smelling petitionary prayers are for *us*, and we would be wise to ask them to offer such prayers on our behalf, as they most willingly do, and indeed, as God sometimes even answers in the form of miracles.

So then, we should pray regularly to the saints — to our favorite saints, to patron saints of our vocations or special interests, to saints of our nation or lands of our heritage, to saints of religious orders dear to our hearts, to saints we are named after and whose names we have chosen for Confirmation, and, if we suffer from physical or mental ailments, to the bevy of saints who have become patrons of the afflicted, from St. Peregrine Laziosi (1265–1345) for those suffering with cancer, to St. Dymphna (seventh century) for those suffering from depression or other mental illness, to St. Rita of Cascia (1381–1457), a patron saint of the lonely. We can also pray some of the many prayers composed *by* saints.

My small Latin Mass missalette includes, for example, traditional prayers from St. Ambrose and our own St. Thomas Aquinas to help prepare for Mass. Many prayers of the saints are of extraordinary beauty. In our previous chapter, we mentioned St. Thomas's prayer that gave rise to the beautiful sung version of the "Panis Angelicus." Other remarkably beautiful prayers include St. Francis of Assisi's "Canticle of the Sun." There is another prayer that comes to mind, from the patron saint of Ireland, that I'd like to quote at some length, but I'll do so in our next chapter. When you read it (and pray it) you'll know why!

I'll conclude this section by noting that not only have saints composed prayers of their own, but some have provided us with very interesting and powerful *ways* to pray, using various postures that truly honor God in mind, soul, and body. A noteworthy example is the Nine Ways of Prayer[117] practiced by St. Dominic de Guzman (1170–1221), the founder of the Order of Preachers, which so captivated St. Thomas.

Saints of the Sacraments and the Holy Mass

The sacraments strengthened all the saints in the same ways they can strengthen us. Some saints are even known for their devotion to a particular sacrament. Take, for the most obvious example, St. John the Baptist! The designation of saints as "confessors" does not denote the sacrament of Penance or Confession, but

---

[117] "Nine Ways of Prayer," Dominicans of St. Cecilia, https://www.nashvilledominican.org/our-vowed-life/st-dominic/nine-ways-of-prayer/.

rather, saints who boldly and publicly professed or confessed the Faith despite imprisonment or other hardships yet did not suffer martyrdom. Still, there are some saints who were priests who were indeed known as masters of the sacrament of Penance, whom people of their time sought out for their spiritual guidance. St. Thomas's teacher, St. Albert the Great, was one example of a saint who preached the importance of Confession: "He is truly zealous for souls who by holy contemplation and fervent desire, by tears and prayers, by night-watchings and fasts, by preaching and hearing of confessions, by wise counsel, salutary correction, and other good works labors for the salvation of souls."[118] And among saints known for healing souls through hearing confessions for as many as twelve or more hours per day are St. John Vianney (1786-1859), St. Joseph Caffaso (1811–1860), St. Leopold Mandic (1866–1942), and St. Padre Pio (1887–1968).

Further, though all saints cherish the Eucharist, some are known to have experienced intense periods of mystical ecstasy after receiving Christ in Communion. St. Catherine of Siena, for example, experienced mystical visions and ecstasies in public lasting for several hours after receiving Communion, and she lived for long periods near the end of her life on the Eucharist alone. Another is St. Martin de Porres (1579–1639). Friends reported he would often seem to disappear after Holy Communion, only to be found seeking silence and solitude in a variety of hiding places in the priory, including in dank basements and even up on the roof. There, in ecstasy, he would contemplate the Body, Blood, Soul, and Divinity of Christ, who had given Himself to Him. Indeed, Martin himself never spoke of his ecstasies, and

---

[118] St. Albert the Great, cited in St. Albert's College, ed., *Saint Albertus Magnus* (Racine, WI.; Saint Catherine's Press, 1938), vii.

some biographers have opined that his superiors encouraged him not do so, lest he be suspected of heresy and brought before the Inquisition!

There is perhaps no other saint who has *written about* the sacrament of the Eucharist in a more lofty, penetrating, theological manner, and in a most beautiful, personally devout way as well, as our own St. Thomas Aquinas, both the Church's ultimate authority on *transubstantiation* and the author of lyrical hymns such as "Adoro Te Devote, Latens Deitas" (Devoutly I Adore Thee, Hidden Deity). We will look at both in our last chapter, but for now, let's draw our attention to the crucial role the saints play in the greatest of all prayers of the Church and the holiest of all rites that make up the Holy Sacrifice of the Mass.

Please take just a moment to reflect: Can you think of examples of the presence of the saints in the rites of the Holy Mass? How many come to mind? Well, I don't claim this list is exhaustive, but here are perhaps a surprising number of instances in both forms of the Mass:

- The Penitential Rite of the new form of the Mass asks for the prayers of the Virgin Mary and all the angels and saints, and the Confiteor of the old form confesses to the Virgin Mary, St. Michael the Archangel, John the Baptist, the apostles Peter and Paul, all the saints, and then names them all again in asking for their prayers.

- In the Old Mass, after the priest goes up to the altar, his prayers include mention of the merits of the saints whose relics are in the altar and of all the saints.

- Most of the epistles that are read at Mass were composed by saints, most frequently by St. Paul.

- The Gospel readings were written, of course, by the four saintly Evangelists: Matthew, Mark, Luke, and John.

- Although the Credo, or Nicene Creed, does not mention saints by name, it does note the fourth mark of the Church as "apostolic," harking back to Christ's first chosen apostles, eleven of whom are saints.
- When the Apostles' Creed is sometimes substituted for the Nicene Creed in the new form of the Mass, we specifically profess our faith in "the communion of saints."
- Whenever the altar is incensed, it recalls the Mass in heaven with those "golden bowls full of incense, which are the prayers of the saints" (Rev. 5:8).
- In the *Suscipe Sancta Trinitas* (Prayer to the Most Holy Trinity) of the Latin Mass, the priest prays to God, commemorates Christ, and notes that the oblation of the Mass also honors the Virgin Mary, as well as Sts. John the Baptist, Peter and Paul, and all the saints.
- The *Communicantes* (Invocation of the Saints) in the canon of the Old Mass honors the memory of the Virgin Mother Mary, St. Joseph, and mentions various apostles and martyrs, both from apostolic times and from the early centuries of the Church.[119] The corresponding Eucharistic

---

[119] They are Peter and Paul (named together as joint founders of the Church), Andrew, James, John, Thomas, James, Philip, Bartholomew, Matthew, Simon and Thaddeus (Apostles); Linus, Cletus, Clement (all bishops of Rome ordained by Peter), Sixtus (Sixtus II, another early pope, whose deacon was St. Lawrence), Cornelius (an early martyred pope), Cyprian (martyred bishop of Carthage in North Africa), Lawrence (martyred deacon), Chrysogonus (martyred under Emperor Diocletian), John and Paul (martyred under Emperor Julian the Apostate), and Cosmas and Damian (twin physicians martyred under Diocletian whose remains are in Rome).

Prayers of the New Mass also include an invocation of saints with truncated lists of their names.

- After the Consecration, the priest invokes the intercession of a variety of apostles and martyrs, including some female martyrs (Felicitas, Perpetua, Agatha, Lucy, Cecilia, and Anastasia) in expression of our hope that someday we might join them in heaven.
- Traditional prayers immediately following the conclusion of the Latin Mass (called Leonine Prayers, after Pope Leo XIII), include prayers to and by saints: the Hail Mary; the Salve Regina (Hail Holy Queen); a prayer based on Psalm 46 [45]:1 — "God is our refuge and our strength" — which invokes the intercession of the Virgin Mother Mary and all the saints; and the prayer to St. Michael the Archangel.

A quick tour of the Mass like this one should be sufficient to show that saints form an integral part of our Faith. Indeed, Christ came that we might take up our crosses, follow Him, and join their number.

LIFE LESSON 11 SUMMA

Be a saint! We can reach no higher, and God expects no less of us. Though all of us are sinners, God has given us countless graces to help us rise above sin, all the way to heaven. Among those generous gifts are the examples and the intercessions of the Church Triumphant in heaven, that holy communion of saints of both sexes, all ages, and all regions of the earth. We must cast off the presumption that we do not need their aid and the despair that falsely claims that they cannot help us. May we be lifted up by their examples and inspired to display heroic virtues of our own in how we think, do, and love. May we pray *to* the saints for their intercession, pray *like* the saints in their holy love for God, and pray at times *in the very words* great saints have given us, especially as we gather together with each other, with them, and with the angels at the Holy Sacrifice of the Mass. May we pray, as the old spiritual hymn goes, that when the saints go marching in, we may be in their number.

Get Jesus

*Live as if Jesus truly is your way,
your truth, and your life.*

How is Jesus "the way, and the truth, and the life?"

Thomas answers that ...

"The way, it has been said, is Christ himself, so he says, 'I am the way.' This is indeed true, for, as stated in Romans (Rom. 5:2), it is through him that we have access to the Father. . . . Because this way is not separated from its destination but united to it, he adds, 'and the truth, and the life.' So Christ is at once both the way and the destination. He is the way by reason of his human nature, and the destination because of his divinity. Therefore, as human, he says, 'I am the way"; as God, he adds, 'and the truth, and the life.' "

—St. Thomas Aquinas, *Commentary on the Gospel of John*, chapter14, lecture 2

The Way

During my years in the atheistic wilderness, I so admired a quotation from atheist philosopher Friedrich Nietzsche's (1844–1900) *Thus Spoke Zarathustra* that I included it in an early book I wrote about strength training and bodybuilding. It ran as follows:

This is my way; where is yours — thus I answered those who asked me "the way." For the way — that does not exist.

That was quite a heady saying from the pen of the son of a Lutheran minister and quite a shame that it struck this poorly catechized young Catholic as so profound. It wasn't until my early forties that I encountered a much more sublime and "angelic" philosopher who showed me that "the way" really, truly does exist, and His name is Jesus Christ!

Nietzsche's professed lack of any one way truly struck a chord with the burgeoning modernist mind and continues to help to deform it in our day. If it reminds you of the all-too-common moral relativism of our day, you are all too correct. Nietzsche wrote in the late 1800s that the most profound line in the whole Bible was Pontius Pilate's question to Christ, "What is truth?" (John 18:38). In our day, many modern people effectively combine both of Nietzsche's misguided insights as they boldly declare the absolute doctrine of relativism: "This is my truth; where is yours? For the truth — that does not exist." Setting aside what should be the obvious self-contradiction — in that to declare there is *no* objective truth is in itself a declaration that one's statement is *true* — this idea is alive, though unwell, and widespread in these turbulent times, times in which so many have lost *their* way precisely because they have lost *the* way.

Got *All* of Jesus?

At the same time atheistic thinkers were disparaging and discarding the way of Christ, modern thinkers within the Church were increasingly discarding the *parts* of Christ that did not line up well with *their way* of thinking. In the early twentieth century, some modernist theologians, both inside and outside the Catholic Church, discarded their belief in the supernatural and the miraculous and sought for a "historical Jesus" who was essentially only a man and a great moral teacher. In a sense, this was nothing new. The Church had battled the Arian heresy, which denied Christ's divinity, back in the fourth century. Others, then and in our time, may not openly question Christ's divinity but seek to shape His teachings to fit their ways of thinking, discarding "harsh sayings" or "truth bombs," as they are sometimes called, from His moral lessons, such as the need to repent of sins *at the risk of hell*, or the indissolubility of marriage, or Christ's deep mystical teaching that we must eat His Flesh and drink His Blood to have eternal life. Modernists teach a soft, malleable Christ who is quite content to let us do our own thing as we define and redefine our own ways. We can see their divisive fruits in the ever-growing fragmentation of Protestant sects and in some sectors within the Catholic Church where every moral and theological teaching would seem to be up for grabs by our modern, enlightened minds.

Some devout Christians of various persuasions in our time ask the simple question, so pithy and apt for bumper stickers—*Got Jesus?* Well, I believe St. Thomas "got Jesus," all of Jesus, in His fullness, like few people before him or since, making him a most valuable guide to living out our last life lesson of really getting Jesus.

The Alpha and the Omega

Jesus said He is "the Alpha and the Omega," the A and the Z, the beginning and the end (Rev. 1:8; 21:6; 22:13). Thomas crafted his *Summa Theologica* with this profound theme in mind. The three major "parts" are devoted to God, man, and Christ, respectively, and are interrelated in an overarching *exitus-reditus* (out from God, back to God) theme. From God flows all creation, including man, who is made in His image and likeness. This is the stuff of Part I. Part II (subdivided into two smaller parts: I-II and II-II), focuses on man's journey back to God through an examination of moral living and virtue. Part III completes man's ultimate return to God via the way, who is Christ and the Church He established. Here is a simple graphic:

Part I
Of God, and the
Outflowing of His
Creation

Part II
Of Man, the Rational
Creature, and His
Return to God

Part III
Of Christ, Who, as
Man, Is Our Way
to God

    You might note a parallel with this book's life lessons. Life lesson one, on accepting only the best, made clear from the very beginning that our final end or goal is to get back to the God who made us and to share in eternal life with Him. Life lessons two through eleven examine ten key things we can do while on earth to fulfill that goal and get back to God. This chapter's last life lesson addresses the final, ultimate, necessary means to reach our goal of God in heaven by embracing God the Savior, who came down to earth for our sake. This pattern, like the words of Scripture, also reveals that the Jesus Christ of our last life lesson, our *Omega* so to speak, was also our *Alpha*, right there at the beginning. When we get back to God, through Christ, we get back to Christ as well, since "In the beginning was the Word and the Word was with God, and the Word was God. He was in the beginning with God; all things were made through him, and without him was not anything made that was made" (John 1:1–3). To see Christ only as a man is to fail to see the Word who is God, to miss both the Alpha and the Omega. Indeed, as St. Thomas wrote so well, in our introductory quotation, Christ is not only the way, but the *destination*! Let's turn to Thomas, then, for some insights on how we can embrace *the way and the destination* with a human face who can lead us to the divine face of God.

The King Who Conquered the Queen of the Vices

We have looked briefly at Christ as the way (and the destination) through our clear Thomistic lenses. Of course, Christ declared that His is not only the way, but also "the truth and the life" (John 14:6). Thomas wrote that Christ lived the kind of life He did on earth to fulfill the three main ends of his Incarnation.

1. He came to proclaim the truth: "He says Himself (John 18:27): *"For this I was born, and for this I came into the world, that I should give testimony to the truth."* For that reason, he lived a social, public life, interacting with and teaching others.

2. Secondly, says Thomas, Christ came to free us from sin: "According to 1 Tim. 1:35: *Christ Jesus came into the world to save sinners*" (III, 40, 1). Therefore, Christ did not live a solitary life, but as St. John Chrysostom notes, Christ went out in search of sinners like a shepherd searching for lost sheep or a physician making his rounds.

3. "He came that by Him *we might have access to God*, as
it is written (Rom. 5:2)" (III, 40, 1).[120]

Christ came both to show us the good news of His truth and
to help us pulverize the sins that keep us from His truth. Since He
searches like a shepherd for us lost sheep, it would behoove us to
cry out "Baa!" to Him and seek Him out as well. Since He comes
to us like a physician making his rounds, it would behoove us to
follow His prescription when He tells us, as He told the woman
caught in adultery, "Do not sin again" (John 8:11).

Aristotle once said that as virtues hone in on the bull's-eye
and hit the target square on, there are many ways, through a
myriad of vices and sins, that we can miss it by a mile. In our
previous sections on sin for each of our life lessons, we've seen
many examples of the kinds of sins that can draw us away from
the target of limited happiness on earth and total bliss with God
in heaven.

We have seen, too, how Thomas, following Pope St. Gregory the Great, notes that the seven capital vices of sloth, envy,
avarice, vainglory, gluttony, lust, and wrath, are particularly
"deadly" because they can lead us to the kinds of mortal sins
that bring death to the soul, and yet the two great saints considered one vice even more deadly than the "seven deadly sins,"
since it can give birth to all seven and all of their progeny too.
This they called "the queen of the vices," and this queen's
name is Pride.

Pride has been with us here on earth since Adam and Eve
chose to follow their desires rather than the will of God, but

---

[120] The full verse reads as follows: "Through him we have obtained
access to this grace in which we stand, and we rejoice in our
hope of sharing the glory of God" (Rom. 5:2).

it existed even before that in heaven when Satan declared to God, *"Non serviam!"* (I will not serve!) In our day, though, pride is attaining a very powerful ascendancy where formerly Christian cultures are becoming increasingly secularized. Man is, in essence, increasingly consciously choosing himself over God, enthroning his own will, and casting God aside as irrelevant or nonexistent.

Lust, for example, deriving from our natural desires for the procreation of the species, has been with us always and has always required struggle and restraint. But now, as never before, popular culture and media, and indeed, even some Christian religious denominations, glorify lust and strive to promote and sell every form of sexual sin as a proper expression of our sexuality, regardless of the damage to countless families and to the destruction of millions of unborn children through the abortion industry, which profits from sins against chastity by charging fees for violations of the fifth commandment. Ignorance and weakness certainly play a role here, which is why young would-be mothers and fathers facing an unexpected pregnancy need to be educated, supported, loved, and shown the value of every life. Their ignorance and weakness would not result in a death, however, if it were not for the educated and powerful providers of abortion, who willfully decide that they, and not God, are the arbiters of the value or lack thereof, of a human life. The whole modern Culture of Death, as Pope St. John Paul II called it, could not survive without the pride of its promoters and profiteers.

Any sins become far more deadly when openly flaunted through pride, but Christ came as a King who conquered the queen of the vices along with the Lord of Hell, who tries to keep her enthroned in our hearts. He would have us do the same, and

He told us how two virtues above all others can help us conquer all kinds of sins.

The Ultimate in Godly Virtues and Gifts

We saw in chapter 11 how every canonized saint displayed heroic virtues in the service of God and neighbor. Of course, *the main reason we should imitate saints is that they became saintly and virtuous by imitating Christ.* They help us imitate Christ by showing us how a Christ-centered life is possible anywhere in the world, at any time in history. So, wherever we are sitting, and whenever we happen to read this, Christ calls out to you and me, as He did to all the saints, to take up our crosses and follow Him to heaven. The crosses we bear will elicit all manner of virtues, but let's zoom in again on two virtues above all others that Christ not only extols but desires to help us acquire.

Jesus extols *humility*. St. Paul wrote that Christ "humbled himself and became obedient to death, even death on a cross" (Phil. 2:8). Jesus declared, "Take my yoke upon you, and learn from me; for I am gentle and lowly in heart, and you will find rest for your souls. For my yoke is easy and my burden light" (Matt. 11:29–30). We have seen already how humility, lowliness of heart, is the foundation of appropriate self-love, a love that recognizes both the limits of our own sinfulness and the limitless power of God's graces, so that we can do all things through Christ, who strengthens us (see Phil. 4:13).

Humility is *meek* in counting others better than ourselves, in turning the other cheek when insulted, in giving our cloak as well to the person who wants our coat. Indeed, "blessed are the meek, for they shall inherit the earth" (Matt. 5:5). Though *meek*, the virtue of humility is anything but *weak*. Christ, though humble and meek, showed unequalled manly fortitude in bearing the physical pains of His Crucifixion, and in His forceful display of righteous indignation in driving the money-changers from the Temple with a whip of chords when they had turned his "Father's house into a house of trade" (John 2:16).

If *humility* is the lowly but sturdy foundation of the cathedral of virtue, *charity* is the crowning cross at its apex. Jesus showed His humility in taking on our humanity; He remained fully God all the while, and as St. John makes clear, "God is love" (1 John 4:16). Here again, we recall from our second life lesson how Thomas explained that Jesus' law is the *law of love*; how in our fifth life lesson we saw how St. Aelred explained that Christ's yoke is *the yoke of charity*, which makes our brother's and sister's burdens light for us; and how we saw in life lesson seven that our love must always go out to sinners. Christ, the God who is love, can *truly* be found in some *way* in every one our twelve Thomistic *life* lessons, since Thomas knew so well that Christ is indeed "*Via, Veritas, et Vita*" (the way, the truth, and the life).

We should bear in mind, too, that while Christ in His humanity perfected every virtue, Isaiah prophesized: "There shall come forth a shoot from the stump of Jesse, and a branch shall grow out of his roots. And the Spirit of the LORD shall rest upon him, and the spirit of wisdom and understanding, the spirit of counsel and might, the spirit of knowledge and the fear of the Lord. And his delight shall be in the fear of the LORD" (Isa. 11:1–3). Isaiah prophesized how Jesus Christ would receive most completely the seven spiritual gifts of the Holy Spirit. Recall that, through virtues, our wills and passions are guided by right human reason. When we open ourselves to the workings of the gifts of the Holy Spirit, we are guided by the divine stirrings of the Holy Spirit Himself. Christ had both a human will and a divine omnipotent will, and they were always completely aligned (III, 18), making Him the ultimate model of the complete and harmonious utilization of the virtues and the gifts.

Talking to Christ in His Words and in Our Own

We have already considered aplenty in these pages the words Christ gave us to pray in the Our Father, but He provided many other lessons for us on prayer too, both in His words and in His actions. Thomas wrote a question of four articles entitled "Of Christ's Prayer" (III, 21). In the first article, he explains how it was "becoming" or fitting for Christ to pray because "the Divine and human wills are distinct in Christ, and the human will of itself is not efficacious enough to do what it wishes, except by Divine power, hence to pray belongs to Christ as man and as having a human will" (III, 21, 1). If Christ's human will needed prayer, how much more does our own!

In addressing another issue quite relevant to our prayer lives, Thomas notes in the third article that while Christ prayed for others, He also prayed for Himself, and He did so in two ways. When He prayed in the Garden of Gethsemane that the chalice of His Passion might pass from Him (Matt. 26:39), He expressed the desire of his sensual nature and simple will as a human being. When He prayed for the glory of His Resurrection (John 17:1), he expressed the desire of His deliberate will guided by reason. Thomas explains that Jesus prayed to His Father to provide us an example of prayer and of the fact that His Father is the author of both His human and His eternal divine natures. Jesus also prayed to give thanks for what He had received in His human nature (Matt. 26:27; John 11:41) and prayers that include petitions for gifts He had not yet received in His human nature, such as the glory of His body (John 17:1).

Per Thomas: "And in this He gave us an example, that we should give thanks for the benefits received, and ask in prayer for those we have not as yet."

As for that prayer to the Father in the garden in which Christ asked that the chalice of His Passion might pass from Him, we will recall that He immediately followed with "nevertheless, not as I will, but as thou wilt" (Matt. 26:39). This raises interesting questions if Christ's human and divine wills are perfectly aligned, and Thomas provides several interesting answers from Sts. Hilary, Jerome, Dionysius of Alexandria, Ambrose, Augustine, and John Chrysostom.

Thomas concludes that if we understand it according to Hilary, Christ prayed that the chalice might "pass *from* Him" *to* other future martyrs who would imitate Him with unfailing hope, or that He would not be overcome with fear of His Passion, or that death would not hold Him, and in these interpretations, Christ's prayer was indeed completely fulfilled. Ambrose, Augustine, and John Chrysostom agreed that Christ prayed that prayer "*as man*, being reluctant to die according to His natural will." Still, this does not mean that Christ's human and divine wills were not aligned, "because His reason which formed the petition did not desire its fulfillment, but for our instruction, it was His will to make known to us His natural will and the movement of His sensuality, which was His as a man." Further, in the reply to a fourth objection: "When He says, I shall cry and Thou wilt not hear, we must take this as referring to the desire of sensuality, which shunned death. But He is heard as to the desire of His reason, as stated above."

Please note well how even in this intense and sorrowful prayer for Himself, a prayer during which He experienced what physicians call hematidrosis, the sweating of blood (Luke 22:44),

His thoughts also reached out to us, in teaching us how to pray. Thomas considered Christ "the most excellent of teachers," who taught not through His writings, but in "that manner of teaching whereby His doctrines are imprinted on the hearts of His hearers," and "as one having power" through the words and deeds of His life (III, 42, 4, citing Matt. 7:29).

With this idea in mind, if we heed this life lesson and seek to "get Jesus" through prayer, whenever we read the Gospels, we should be on high alert for the many valuable lessons Christ teaches about prayer in His words and deeds, from His days of fasting and prayer in the desert, to His kneeling in prayer in reverence for the Father in the Garden of Gethsemane, to the words He gave us to pray, to His simple words of advice that we should all heed every day: "go into your room and shut the door and pray to your Father who is in secret: and your Father who sees in secret will reward you" (Matt. 6:6).

Of course, we can pray to Christ, as well as to the Father, and I'll close this section with brief excerpts from ancient and beautiful Christ-centered prayers composed by two great saints. The first is attributed to the man who brought the Holy Trinity to the Emerald Isle. Inspired by the words of Isaiah 60:1: "Arise, shine; for your light has come, and the glory of the LORD has risen upon you," our first saint prays as follows:

Christ with me
Christ before me
Christ behind me
Christ in me
Christ beneath me
Christ above me
Christ on my right

Christ on my left
Christ when I lie down
Christ when I sit down
Christ when I arise
Christ in the heart of every man who thinks of me
Christ in the mouth of every one who speaks of me
Christ in every eye that sees me
Christ in every ear that hears me.
I arise today through a mighty strength
the invocation of the Trinity
through belief in the threeness,
through confession of the oneness
of the Creator of Creation.[121]

Our second excerpt from a Christ-centered prayer is from a most angelic saint we all know so well:

Devoutly I adore You, hidden Deity,
Under these appearances concealed.
To You my heart surrenders self
For seeing You, all else must yield....
Jesus, whom I see enveiled,
What I desire, when will it be?
Beholding Your fair face revealed,
Your glory shall I be blessed to see.
Amen.[122]

---

[121] From St. Patrick's elaborate, magnificent "Breastplate" prayer, available in full on many online sites.
[122] The first and last stanzas of *Adoro Te Devote, Latens Deitas* (Devoutly I Adore You, Hidden Deity) in Anderson and Moser, *The Aquinas Prayer Book*, 97.

Feeling God Cleave to Your Innermost Parts

Do you ever hear Christians of various denominations talk about the importance of establishing "a personal relationship with Jesus Christ"? Well, Thomas would agree that is the most important relationship, indeed, the most important thing in all the world and in heaven, the direct goal of our first and last life lessons, and the goal that all of our life lessons serve. When I hear this phrase from non-Catholics, my thoughts often go to our great communion of saints. Every one of our canonized saints has established a relationship with Christ in the most profound and personal way. Still, there is another sense in which all of us as Catholics are blessed to establish a "personal relationship with Jesus Christ," indeed, to "get Jesus," indeed, *all* of Jesus, in a most miraculous and intimate way, a way that Christ Himself established for us, a way that every ordained priest makes available to us while acting in the person of Christ in a mysterious way that exceeds our understanding but has been explained as sublimely as humanly possible by our own Angelic Doctor.

The "hidden Deity" to whom Thomas prays, the Deity present in such a way that "sight and touch and taste here fail; hearing only can be believed,"[123] is the Body, Blood, Soul, and Divinity of Christ, truly present in the sacrament of the Eucharist. In the hymns he composed for the feast of Corpus Christi, Thomas is

---

[123] Ibid, 69. The "hearing" Thomas refers to refers primarily to the "hard saying" of the words that Christ spoke to His disciples in the "bread of life" narrative in John 6; for example, "He who eats my flesh and drinks my blood has eternal life" (v. 54) and Christ's words on the institution of the Eucharist at the Last Supper (Matt. 26:26–28; Mark 14:22–15; Luke 22:14–20), recapitulated by St. Paul (1 Cor. 11: 24–25) and at every Catholic Mass at the Consecration of the Eucharist.

the elegant poet of the Eucharist, and in the *Summa Theologica*, III, 73-83, he is its sublime theologian, indeed, the "Eucharistic Doctor." Thomas wrote nearly a hundred pages on the Eucharist in the *Summa* (in double-column print), and I hope you'll peruse them someday. For now, we'll take just a few peeks to give you a taste of his nuggets of wisdom.

In question 74, Thomas addresses the ostensibly mundane issue of the material elements of the Eucharist and provides us insights such as these:

> It is appropriate that bread and wine are used in this sacrament because Christ himself instituted the sacrament with bread and wine (Matt. 26). And as for four more figurative reasons: (1) water is used in Baptism for spiritual cleansing, and since the Eucharist feeds us spiritually, bread and drink are appropriate, (2) during Christ's Passion his blood was separated from his body, and in the Eucharist "the bread is received apart as the sacrament of the body and the wine as the sacrament of the blood," (3) in terms of effect, as St. Ambrose wrote, *"Christ's body is offered* under the species of bread *for the health of the body; and the blood* under the species of wine *for the health of the soul,* according to Lev. 17:14; *The life of the animal* (Vulgate—*of all flesh) is in the blood,* and (4), as to the effect with regard to the whole Church, which is made up of many believers, just as bread is composed of many grains, and wine flows from many grapes, as the gloss observes on 1 Cor. 10:17: We being many are ... one body, etc." (74, 1)

> Further, Christ has compared himself both to a grain of wheat (John 12:24) and to the vine (John 15:1; cited in 74, 2).

Water is mixed with the wine because Christ probably did so in keeping with the Jewish custom of the time; "hence it is written (Prov. 9:5): *Drink the wine I have mixed for you.*" Further, Pope Alexander I emphasized that both blood and water flowed from Christ's side in the Passion, and Pope Julius wrote "*the people are signified by the water, but Christ's blood by the wine. Therefore when water is mixed with the wine in the chalice, the people is made one with Christ.*" Moreover, St. Ambrose wrote of another "effect of this sacrament, which is the entering into everlasting life; hence: *The water flows into the chalice, and springs forth unto everlasting life.*" Ambrose also noted that while the Eucharist was prefigured by Melchisedech's offering of bread and wine, "so likewise it is signified by the water which flowed from the rock in the desert according to 1 Cor. 10:4: *But they drank of the spiritual rock which came after them.*" Finally, the water of baptism absolves while the water of the Eucharist refreshes "according to Psalm 22:3: *He hath brought me up on the water of refreshment*, and since bread is made with water and flour, "therefore, since water is mixed with the wine, neither is without the water." (74, 6)

In the following nine questions of seventy articles, Thomas really gets into the heart and the soul (not to mention the Body, Blood, and Divinity) of the sacrament of the Eucharist. I'll provide here merely the tersest of summaries of a few of the most striking highlights.

Thomas makes crystal clear, through multiple arguments from Scripture and the Church Fathers, that the body of Christ is in the sacrament of the Eucharist "in very truth," and not "merely as in a figure or sign." He cites Berengarius of Tours (ca. 999–1088) as the first to devise the heresy that Christ's Body and Blood are present in the Eucharist only as a spiritual sign (a belief now held by most non-Catholic Christians, and indeed by some within the Church). Among more intriguing, moving defenses of Christ's Real Presence, Thomas cites Matthew, John — and Aristotle! Recall that Christ told us while on earth, "No longer do I call you servants, for the servant does not know what the master is doing; but I have called you friends" (John 15:15). Aristotle wrote that a special feature of friendship is that friends live together. Thomas notes that Christ promised His bodily presence to us as a reward at the close of the age, "saying (Matt. 24:28): *Where the body is, there shall the eagles be gathered together.*" Still, even during our pilgrimage on earth He provides us with His bodily presence through the Eucharist. In John 6:57 "he says: *He that eateth My flesh and drinketh My blood, abideth in Me, and I in him.* Hence, this sacrament is the sign of extreme charity, and the uplifter of our hope, from such familiar union of Christ with us" (III, 75, 1).

In II, 75, 4–8, Thomas describes the miracle of *transubstantiation*, whereby in the sacrament of the Eucharist the *substance* of the bread and wine is changed into the Body, Blood, Soul, and Divinity of Christ, while the *accidents* of the bread and wine, perceptible by our senses, continue to remain. As he noted in the first article of this question, "The presence of Christ's true body and blood in this sacrament cannot be detected by sense, nor understanding, but by faith alone, which rests upon Divine authority. Hence, on Luke 22:19: *This is My body, which shall be delivered up for you,* Cyril says: *Doubt not whether this be true: but take rather the Saviour's words with faith, since He is the Truth, He lieth not.*" In the fourth article, Thomas reminds doubters of the Real Presence, that while "every change wrought by nature entails a change in a particular thing's form, God's power is infinite, hence His action extends to the whole nature of being. Therefore, He can work not only formal conversion, so that diverse forms succeed each other in the same subject; but also the change of all being, so that, to wit, the whole substance of one thing can be changed into the whole substance of another" … as "the whole substance of bread is changed into the whole substance of Christ's body, and the whole substance of the wine into the whole substance of Christ's blood."

Question 79 treats "Of the Effects of This Sacrament" in a full eight articles. These effects include the bestowal of grace, the attainment of glory, the forgiveness of venial sins, fortification against future sins, and, because this sacrament is also a sacrifice (recall our chapter on the Mass), the Eucharist also benefits others who do not receive it, because to them "it is beneficial by way of sacrifice, inasmuch as it is offered for their salvation." Thomas notes that the fact that the Eucharist does not forgive mortal sins is made clear in the words of St. Paul. "It is written (1 Cor. 11:29): *He that eateth and drinketh unworthily, eateth and drinketh judgment to himself*; and a gloss of the same passage makes the following commentary: *He eats and drinks unworthily who is in the state of sin, or who handles (the sacrament) irreverently; and such a one eats and drinks judgement, i.e., damnation unto himself.*" May these words remind us to show the greatest reverence to the Eucharist and, if we are stained by mortal sin, to avail ourselves of the sacrament of Confession before we receive Communion.

In the sixth article of question 80, Thomas addresses head-on "Whether the Priest Ought to Deny the Body of Christ to the Sinner Seeking It." Citing Augustine on the fact that all of us are sinners, the answer to that question in general is no. However, "a distinction must be made among sinners: some are secret; others are notorious, either from evidence of the fact, as public usurers, or public robbers, or from being denounced as evil men by some ecclesiastical or civil tribunal. Therefore, Holy Communion ought not to be given to open sinners when they ask for it." How relevant a statement for our turbulent times when self-proclaimed Catholic politicians who promote abortion of the unborn, and recently even death through neglect of the newly born children who survive attempted abortions, line up to receive the Holy Eucharist. Thankfully, some priests and bishops are aware of this important life lesson from St. Thomas Aquinas.[124]

LIFE LESSON 12 SUMMA

To "get Jesus" then, we must learn about Jesus through the Gospels and the teachings of the Church, fight against sin with His aid, build virtues and employ the Holy Spirit's gifts as He modeled so perfectly for us, pray for His assistance in the words and ways He taught us, and partake worthily of the Eucharist, so that Jesus might abide in us, and we in Him, as He wants us to. Finally, may each one of us pray after every Communion, like the priest in the Traditional Latin Mass, that Christ's Body and Blood that we have received will *"adhaeret visceribus meis"* (cleave to my innermost parts).

---

[124] I cannot help but point out the injustice here on the part of pro-abortion politicians who seek to continue to receive Communion. Christ told us to do unto others as we would have them do unto us. Abortion prevents the unborn child from ever having even a First Communion.

Conclusion

Out of the Church
and Into the World

*And Jesus coming, spoke to them saying: All power
is given me in heaven and in earth. Going therefore,
teach ye all nations; baptizing them in the name of
the Father and of the Son, and of the Holy Ghost.
Teaching them to observe all things whatsoever I
have commanded you. And behold I am with you
all days, even to the consummation of the world.*

—Matthew 28:18–20[125]

*"Going therefore to teach all nations." Here He en-
joins their duty; and He enjoins a threefold duty.
Firstly, He enjoins the duty of teaching; secondly
He enjoins the duty of baptizing; and thirdly, He enjoins the duty of instructing regarding morals.*

—St. Thomas Aquinas[126]

The Church and the World in Our Turbulent Times

These are certainly turbulent times both inside and outside the
Church. As scandalous stories seem to break in the news almost
daily, I cannot guess what new crises we may face by the time this

---

[125] Translation in St. Thomas Aquinas, *Commentary of the Gospel of
St. Matthew*, trans. Rev. Paul M. Kimball (n.p.: Dolorosa Press,
2012), 949.

[126] Ibid., 963.

book comes out in print. Such crises are bound to arise to the extent to which we abandon timeless spiritual wisdom in favor of the modern worldly wisdom of our own age. In the aftermath of the tumultuous decades in the Church after Vatican II, decades that cast off so much sacred tradition and experimented with so much man-crafted novelty, raw statistics such as those we cited in our preface showed the proof of the following quip: "A Catholic aphorist put it thus, 'The Mass reforms wished to open the doors of the Church to those who found themselves outside; instead, those who were inside ran out.'"[127]

We might think of some of the modern reforms of the 1960s to the 1980s especially, not only in terms of the Mass, in which the Novus Ordo was sometimes celebrated in strange and less than sacred ways, but also in new church buildings. Churches of great verticality that drew one's eyes up toward heaven were replaced by churches on more horizontal or even more circular plans that draw our eyes toward ourselves.

In so many churches, beautiful painted, stained-glass, and sculptured images of the saints and the angels suffered the fate of iconoclasm and were removed from their pedestals and stored in church basements. And indeed, while massive crucifixes, life-size or greater, once drew all eyes to the summits of high altars, in some churches today, all you might find, if you put on your glasses, is a portable crucifix with a corpus of Christ that might almost fit in your hand. True, He willingly became small for us within Mary's womb, but must *we* make Him small for us? Surely, many modern liturgists reasoned that wise and mature "contemporary" men and woman do not need such distractions, such childish

---

[127] Martin Mosebach, *Subversive Catholicism: Papacy, Liturgy, Church* (Brooklyn, NY: Angelico Press, 2019), 77.

reminders of holiness, perhaps forgetting or completely unaware that a very wise, mature man contemporary to his own age wrote of the timeless necessity of visible icons of holiness because "it is part of man's nature to acquire knowledge of the intelligible from the sensible" (III, 60, 4). Further:

> Now the reason for the necessity of finding these illustrations or images, is that simple and spiritual impressions easily slip from the mind, unless they be tied as it were to some corporeal image, because human knowledge has a greater hold on sensible objects. (II-II, 49, 1)

Indeed, while some might still consider such images childish, Thomas wrote that the capacity for being awed by striking images "explains why we remember better what we saw when we were children," and Christ Himself declared: "Truly, I say to you, unless you turn and become like children, you will never enter the kingdom of heaven" (Matt. 18:3).

Regardless of the recent rampant denuding and even demolition of churches, and the hemorrhaging of Church members in the Western world, we must never forget that Christ told us He is always with us "even to the consummation of the world." He is always there to help us recapture our childlike capacities for awe, reverence, and love. He ardently desires to give rebirth to our souls, our Church, and our nations. He *does* want those of us inside churches to run out into the world, not to abandon His house, but to go forth with the lessons we learned there, and perhaps through our words and the example of how we live our lives, to bring others in the world back into church with us. We should breathe in great draughts of heavenly oxygen every time we are at Mass and share it with a world that is suffocating.

Sharing and Teaching Timeless,
Eternal Life Lessons

Thomas said that true mastery of knowledge is demonstrated by a person's capacity to teach. If we are to share Thomas's eternal life lessons and help rebuild our families, our communities, our nations, and our Church, we must master them first in our own hearts and minds, by learning them "by heart," so we can contemplate them with our minds whenever we make time to do so.

In the second-to-last table of our appendix is a very simple aid for remembering them, gleaned from Thomas's writings on the perfection of memory. As a start on contemplation, I suggest that we also consider how well these life lessons all hang together, supporting and reinforcing each other, through the use of a simple mental image, which I'm pretty sure Thomas would approve of. (And I'm *certain* his teacher St. Albert the Great would!)[128]

St. Thomas's *Summa Theologica* has been compared by commentators to a great Gothic cathedral, so massive, beautiful, and integrated are all its many parts and adornments. Well, we could think of our twelve life lessons as a cathedral too. The cathedral rests upon God Himself as the foundation in our first life lesson. Christ Himself, the way and destination in our last life lesson, is at the apex upon the high altar in image in the form of a crucifix, in His Real Presence, in the consecrated host, and inside our own very bodily temples of the Holy Spirit. In between, in the nave and the sanctuary, we are taught fundamental lessons of the Faith in the prayers, readings, and sermons, moral lessons informing us in how to live in harmony and peace, how to grow

---

[128] In commenting on ancient techniques using locations to help us place mental images of things we strive to remember, St. Albert noted, "Some will place a church."

in justice, fortitude, charity, and all the virtues, as we see the images of saints and angels and hear of them in the words of the Mass. There is a whole world—and heaven—to contemplate there every time we attend Mass, or even just think of our own church, or of one of the great cathedrals.[129]

To contemplate these lessons even more deeply, we have included in these pages a plethora of citations to the exact locations within the *Summa Theologica* and other of Thomas's works to help you dig deeper if you so choose. Indeed, if you dig more deeply into Thomas's writings, you may well uncover a slew of new powerful life lessons to ponder and live!

We saw that Thomas also taught us that "for even as it is better to enlighten than merely to shine, so it is better to give to others the fruits of one's contemplation rather than merely to contemplate" (II-II, 188, 6). Thomas makes clear that we are not to hoard the spiritual truths we glean through contemplation but are to share them freely with others. He knew well we must "be doers of the word, and not hearers only" (James 1:22). While we are to seek eternal life for ourselves, we should do all that we can so that our families, friends, neighbors, and even those we might now count as enemies can share the bliss with us in heaven.

The kinds of fruits we can glean and share with others will depend to some extent on our God-given individual temperaments,

---

[129] I cannot help but note that I sit here proofreading this book's rough draft, written a couple of weeks ago, on April 16, 2019, the day after the devastating destruction by fire of the magnificent Notre Dame Cathedral in Paris, a structure that St. Thomas himself saw during its original construction. I hope and pray that this tragic loss will awaken us to the inestimable spiritual and cultural value of magnificent sacred art and architecture.

vocations, time, and place on earth. Comparing ourselves with each other may be a case of apples and oranges, so to speak, but every single one of us can share and contribute to the great cornucopia of spiritual merit.[130] Thomas shared the exceedingly succulent fruits of his contemplation and the fruits of the Holy Spirit as well.[131] As we strive to share these life lessons, we might ask ourselves what we can do to nourish, refresh, and bring joy to all those around us.

Thomas knew well that we must express the love of our neighbors not merely in word, but in deed. Recall his explication of 1 John 3:18: "The love of our neighbor requires that not only should we be our neighbor's well-wishers, but also his well-doers" (II-II, 32, 5).[132]

Thomas so shared the fruits of his contemplation through such an amazing quantity of writing, teaching, and preaching that it may have cut his own life on earth rather short. He died on earth and was born in heaven on March 7, 1274, at the age of forty-nine. Thomas wrote extensively about *sins* that turn us away from God. He wrote magnificently of the *virtues* and *gifts* that turn us back toward him. He reported that all of his study, contemplation, his works of spoken and written words, were made

---

[130] If I might stretch the "apples and oranges" metaphor for individual differences just a bit more, I'd compare Thomas's fruit to that of a watermelon. It's the largest fruit I can think of. It contains copious quantities of refreshing water and a multitude of seeds that can generate new sources of nourishment!

[131] These fruits, building on Galatians 5:22–23 are listed as charity, joy, peace, patience, kindness, goodness, generosity, gentleness, faithfulness, modesty, self-control, and chastity (CCC 1832).

[132] 1 John 3:18 reads: "Little children, let us not love in words or speech but in deeds and truth."

possible through *prayer*. As the theologian of transubstantiation and the poet of the feast of Corpus Christi, Thomas understood and cherished the Blessed *Sacrament* and the other six sacraments. Finally, we know without a doubt that the words and the deeds of his life were motivated by *love*, first and foremost by the love of God, and through that love, the love of his neighbors, which include you and me, and, of course, for his own "inward man" or "higher self," which was made to enjoy God in eternity—and does.

In Thomas's magnificent writings on the virtues, he acclaimed charity as the highest, as the "mother of the virtues," which forms, shapes, and moves all of the other virtues of the soul. To love God, others, and ourselves with the love of charity, regardless of how turbulent our times might be, is indeed to love God with all that we are and our neighbors as ourselves.

The End (and the End of the Angelic Doctor)

Many people outside the Church, and, alas, some within it, do not see the value of St. Thomas's lessons for our modern times. So many of our modern errors and the crises they have wrought amount to a rejection of Thomistic wisdom by those who thought they saw further and knew better than the Angelic Doctor. Some have even claimed that, before his death, Thomas renounced his own writings. Let's end with a look at a mysterious incident near the end of our saint's life on earth.

On December 6, 1273, Thomas had an ecstatic experience while saying Mass. The revelation he beheld, perhaps a foretaste of the Beatific Vision, was so powerful that Thomas told his friend Brother Reginald that, after what he had seen, he could write no more, since his writings "appeared as straw." Four months later, after a short illness and before his fiftieth birthday, Thomas died on March 7, 1274, at the Cistercian monastery at Fossonova, leaving his great *Summa Theologica* incomplete.

By calling his writings "straw," he did not renounce them. Thomas had written of three degrees of charity. At the first stage, we fight against sin; at the second stage, we focus on the development of virtue; and in the highest and last stage, we seek only union with God. Indeed, it was this schema that inspired our lesson plans including pulverizing sin, practicing virtue, and seeking union with God through prayer and the sacraments. In a vision of Christ near the end of his life, after Christ told Thomas that he'd written well about Him, He asked Thomas what he wanted from Him. His answer was *"Non nisi Te"* (None but You).

Perhaps, in his last days on earth, Thomas had broached that third degree of charity, restless for nothing but what we have cast as our first and last life lessons, restless for anything but union with God. Perhaps the "straw" that was his theological works had been the kindling that fueled the fires of charity that brought him to that exultant state, so soon before he came to the end of his days on earth and came to cherish his ultimate End of life with God in heaven.

May the lessons that helped Thomas attain eternal life help us and our neighbors attain, with God's grace, that same highest and most eternal of all possible goals.

The End

Appendix

Three Things We Must Know to Be Saved

Necessary Things	Expressed in ...
What to believe	The Creed
What to desire	The Lord's Prayer
What to do	The Law

12 Life Lessons from St. Thomas Aquinas

The Fourfold Law

Law of ...	Description
Nature	A natural light God implants in our reason to know what to do and what to avoid
Concupiscence	The law Satan gave man after the Fall that allows our flesh to rebel against reason
Scripture/ Moses/Fear	The law God gave us, through Moses, after the corruption of the natural law by the law of concupiscence, so that we can conquer sin through the fear of the Lord and be led back to works of holiness.
Scripture/Jesus/ Love	The higher law God gave us, through Jesus Christ, to reject evil in our hearts and seek out the good through our love of God.

Threefold Difference in the Two Scriptural Laws

Law of Moses	Law of Jesus
Slaves	Freemen
Temporal rewards	Everlasting rewards
Heavy	Light

Appendix

Top Ten Effects of Charity or Love

Major Fourfold Effects	Six Other Effects
Transformation of the spiritual life	Forgiveness
Faithfulness in keeping the commandments	Light
Confidence in God	Joy
Everlasting life	Peace
	Dignity
	Sons of God

Five Conditions Required for Prayer as Expressed in the Lord's Prayer

Condition	Brief Explanation
Confidence	Prayer should be confident: "Let us go with confidence to the throne of grace" (Heb. 4:16). We can have no greater confidence than the Lord's Prayer, since Christ gave it to us.
Rectitude	Prayer should have the rectitude to ask for the right things that are truly good for us. St. Paul wrote, "We know not what we should pray for as we ought" (see Rom. 8:26). The apostles said to Jesus, "Lord, teach us to pray" (Luke 11:1). It follows that we pray most rightly when we ask for what He taught us to pray for.
Order	Desires should be orderly, and so should prayer, since it expresses desires. The right order is to pray for spiritual goods before carnal goods: "Seek ye first the kingdom of God and His justice, and all these things shall be added to you" (Matt. 6:33, Douay-Rheims), and in the Lord's Prayer we first ask for heavenly things and then for earthly blessings.

Appendix

Condition	Brief Explanation
Devoutness	The unction (consecrated oil) of devotion makes the sacrifice acceptable to God: "In thy name I will lift up my hands, let my soul be filled as with marrow and fatness" (Ps. 62:5–6, Douay-Rheims [RSV = Ps. 63:4-5]). Yet devotion often cools when prayers are too long, so Christ warned: "When you are praying, speak not much" (Matt. 6:7, Douay-Rheims). Further, devotion arises from charity, which is love of God and neighbor, as is expressed in the loving words "Our Father," in praying for each other, by asking God to give "us," and forgive "us."
Humility	Prayer should be humble: "He hath regard to the prayer of the humble" (Ps. 101:18, Douay-Rheims [RSV = Ps. 102:17]), as is seen in the story of the Pharisee and the publican (Luke 18:10–14), and in the words of Judith "The prayer of the humble and the meek hath always pleased Thee" (Judith 9:16, Douay-Rheims). The Lord's Prayer observes such humility because in it we do not presume on our own strength but trust in obtaining all things through God's power.

St. Thomas on the Varieties of Justice[133]

Types of Justice	Description
Distributive	Distributive justice is one of two "subjective parts" of justice — that is, what justice is all about. Distributive justice is the relation between a whole and its parts. It refers to the way in which a community distributes commons goods to each individual.
Commutative	The other subjective part of justice, commutative justice, regards the relation of one part to another. It refers to private individuals and the mutual dealings between them.
Political	Political justice refers to governmental systems and institutions set up for citizens within a *polis* (community) based on natural rights or on legal agreement or consent between private individuals or by public agreement regarding community goods.
General	General justice refers to the virtue by which a person is a good citizen and acts for the welfare of the common good.
Legal	Legal justice is the expression of general justice in the form of laws designed to benefit the common good.

[133] Distributive and commutative justice are defined in *ST*, II-II, Q. 61, art. 1, legal justice in Q. 58. art. 6, particular and domestic justice in art. 7, political justice in Q. 57, art. 2, and metaphorical justice in Q. 58, art. 2.

Appendix

Types of Justice	Description
Particular	Particular justice directs individuals immediately to the good of other individuals.
Domestic	Domestic justice refers to unique, intimate relationships within a household, such as that between husband and wife, or father and son, in which each person is, in a sense, a part of the other.
Metaphorical	Strictly speaking, justice is always social and between persons. Metaphorical justice refers to treating one's principles of action, such as reason and the concupiscible and irascible appetites, as if they were agents of actions themselves. Thus, metaphorically speaking, we can say that in the just person, the appetites obey the commands of reason, rendering reason its rightful due.

12 Life Lessons from St. Thomas Aquinas

Parts of the Virtue of Justice

Integral Parts	Subjective Parts	Potential Parts
Doing good	Commutative justice	Religion, piety
Avoiding evil	Distributive justice	Observance, gratitude
		Vengeance, truth
		Friendliness, liberality

The Hierarchies and Orders of the Angels[134]

Hierarchy	Order	Characteristics
Highest *They contemplate the idea of things in God Himself and have the closest relation to Him.*	Seraphim	*They are most closely united to God, singing per- petual praises around His throne.*
	Cherubim	*They know the divine secrets "super- eminently" through God Himself.*
	Thrones	*They receive judg- ments from God and pass them on to the second hierarchy.*
Middle *They contemplate the idea of things in uni- versal causes and are involved in governing.*	Dominations	*They appoint things that are to be done.*
	Virtues	*They possess the power to carry out what is to be done.*

---

[134] Derived from I, 108.

Hierarchy	Order	Characteristics
	Powers	*They decide how what has been commanded will be carried out by others.*
Lowest *They contemplate the idea of things in their application to particular effects, and they execute God's works.*	Principalities	*They act as rulers, presiding over the government of peoples and kingdoms of the earth.*
	Archangels	*They announce to men great things above the power of reason.*
	Angels	*They announce to men small things within the limits of reason.*

Appendix

Memorize the 12 Life Lessons[135]

Location	Image	Life Lesson
1. Front door	You sign for a package labeled "The Best."	1. Accept only the best.
2. Doormat	Microscope on mat focuses in on a piece of matter.	2. Focus on things that matter the most.
3. Glass panel next to door	You have no peace because a group in the front yard is singing without any harmony.	3. No harmony, no peace!
4. Portrait on wall by door	Your favorite Supreme Court justice is shown walking through his or her own front door.	4. Justice begins at home.

[135] At the suggestion of an author friend (thank you, Tim Moore), I provide this simple summary chart of suggested memory images for the location system I detailed in my previous books *Memorize the Faith!* and *How to Think Like Aquinas.* The method is based, as is so much else in this book, on the writings of St. Thomas Aquinas, in this case II-II, 49, 1, "Whether Memory Is a Part of Prudence." (If I should come to give public talks on this book, I'll be using these very same images in lieu of written notes!) Please note that the foyer illustration (next page) is provided to show the memory location system rather than the exact images we load on them with our imaginations. The fourth location has two people because when first used in *Memorize the Faith!* it housed the Fourth Commandment, to honor your father and mother. If you use your imagination, these locations can be adapted to help you recall any information you should choose to place there.

285

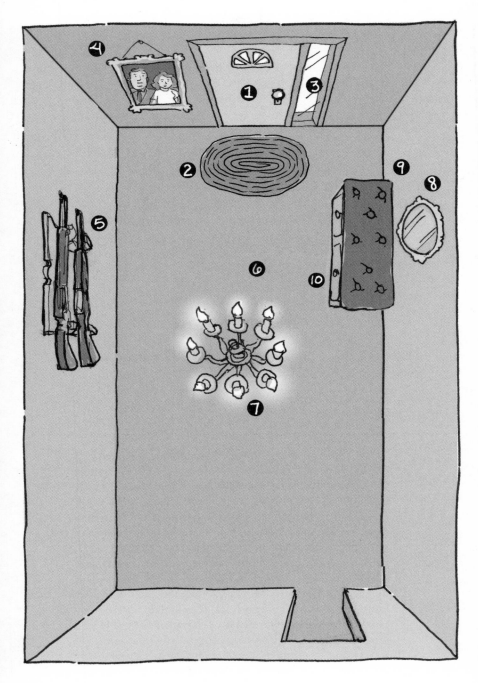

Foyer

Location	Image	Life Lesson
5. Gun rack on side wall	You easily hoist your brothers and sisters on top of the rack.[136]	5. Our brothers (and sisters) ain't heavy.
6. Center of foyer	You smile, greet, and hug your double.	6. Be your own best friend.
7. Chandelier	Jesus is up there writing in sand and telling a woman to go and sin no more, while forgiving her for past sins.	7. Hate the sin, love the sinner.
8. Mirror on other wall	You spy two bees in T-shirts with huge ♂ or ♀ symbols.	8. Be a man (or a woman)!
9. Cushioned bench under mirror	A model of your church sits there surrounded by trees.	9. Go to Mass, not to the woods, every Sunday.
10. Three drawers in bench	As you open the three drawers, out pops your guardian angel, your favorite saint, and Jesus Christ Himself!	10. Listen to that angel on your shoulder 11. Be a saint 12. Get Jesus

[136] Don't have any brothers or sisters? No problem at all. Just imagine them.

12 Life Lessons from St. Thomas Aquinas

12 Life Lessons Thomistic Quotations

Life Lesson	Quotation from St. Thomas Aquinas
1. Accept only the best.	"The ultimate and principal good of man is the enjoyment of God." —*ST*, II-II, 23, 7
2. Focus on things that matter the most.	"Three things are necessary for the salvation of man: to know what he ought to believe; to know what he ought to desire; and to know what he ought to do." —*Treatise on the Two Commandments of Charity*
3. No harmony, no peace!	"Concord denotes union of appetites among various persons, while peace denotes, in addition to this union, the union of the appetites even in one man." —*ST*, II-II, 29, 1
4. Justice begins at home.	"Justice is a habit, which makes a man capable of doing what is just, and of being just in action and in intention." —*ST*, II-II, 58, 1

Appendix

Life Lesson	Quotation from St. Thomas Aquinas
5. Our brothers (and sisters) ain't heavy.	"It is written (Matt 22:39): 'The second commandment is like this: Thou shalt love thy neighbor as thyself.' ... This precept is fittingly expressed, for it indicates both the reason for loving and the mode of love.... Nor does it matter whether we say 'neighbor' or 'brother' according to 1 John 4:21, or 'friend' according to Leviticus 19:18, because all the words express the same affinity." —*ST*, II-II, 44, 7
6. Be your own best friend.	"Just as unity is the principle of union, the love with which a man loves himself is the form and the root of friendship." —*ST*, II-II, 25, 4
7. Hate the sin, love the sinner.	"To correct the wrongdoer is a spiritual alsmdeed. But almsdeeds are works of charity.... Therefore, fraternal correction is an act of charity.... The correction of the wrongdoer is a remedy which should be employed against a man's sin." —*ST*, II-II, 33, 1

Life Lesson	Quotation from St. Thomas Aquinas
8. Be a man (or a woman)!	"Fortitude, as a virtue, perfects the mind in the endurance of all perils whatever; but it does not go so far as to give confidence of overcoming all dangers: this belongs to the fortitude that is the gift of the Holy Spirit." —*ST*, II-II, 139, 1
9. Go to Mass, not to the woods, every Sunday.	"A man is said to be religious from '*religio*,' because he often ponders over, and, as it were, reads again (*religit*), the things which pertain to worship.... Or again, religion may be derived from '*religare*' (to bind together), wherefore Augustine says (*Of True Religion*, 55): May religion bind us to the one Almighty God." —*ST*, II-II, 81, 1
10. Listen to that angel on your shoulder	"There must be some incorporeal creatures. For what is principally intended by God in creatures is good, and this consists in assimilation to God Himself.... Now God produces the creature by his intellect and will. Hence, the perfection of the universe requires that there should be intellectual creatures. Now intelligence cannot be the action of a body, nor of any corporeal faculty limited to here and now. Hence the perfection of the universe requires the existence of an incorporeal creature." —*ST*, I, 50, 1

Life Lesson	Quotation from St. Thomas Aquinas
11. Be a saint	"Do not fail to imitate the lives of saintly and noble men." —*Letter to Brother John on How to Study*
12. Get Jesus	"The way, it has been said, is Christ Himself, so He says, 'I am the way.' This is indeed true, for, as stated in Romans (Rom. 5:2), it is through Him that we have access to the Father.... Because this way is not separated from its destination but united to it, He adds, 'and the truth, and the life.' So Christ is at once both the way and the destination. He is the way by reason of His human nature, and the destination because of His divinity. Therefore, as human, He says, 'I am the way'; as God, He adds, 'and the truth, and the life.'" —*Commentary on the Gospel of John,* chapter14, lecture 2

About the Author

Kevin Vost obtained his Doctor of Psychology in Clinical Psychology from Adler University in Chicago with internship and dissertation research at the Southern Illinois University School of Medicine, Alzheimer's Center, Memory and Aging Clinic.

Dr. Vost has taught psychology and gerontology at Aquinas College in Nashville, the University of Illinois at Springfield, MacMurray College, and Lincoln Land Community College. He has served as a Research Review Committee Member for American Mensa and as an Advisory Board Member for the International Association of Resistance Trainers.

He is the author of nineteen Catholic books, and his hobbies include lifting big weights and reading big books, such as those of St. Thomas Aquinas. He resides with his wife and their two dogs in Springfield, Illinois.

Sophia Institute

Sophia Institute is a nonprofit institution that seeks to nurture the spiritual, moral, and cultural life of souls and to spread the Gospel of Christ in conformity with the authentic teachings of the Roman Catholic Church.

Sophia Institute Press fulfills this mission by offering translations, reprints, and new publications that afford readers a rich source of the enduring wisdom of mankind.

Sophia Institute also operates the popular online resource CatholicExchange.com. *Catholic Exchange* provides world news from a Catholic perspective as well as daily devotionals and articles that will help readers to grow in holiness and live a life consistent with the teachings of the Church.

In 2013, Sophia Institute launched Sophia Institute for Teachers to renew and rebuild Catholic culture through service to Catholic education. With the goal of nurturing the spiritual, moral, and cultural life of souls, and an abiding respect for the role and work of teachers, we strive to provide materials and programs that are at once enlightening to the mind and ennobling to the heart; faithful and complete, as well as useful and practical.

Sophia Institute gratefully recognizes the Solidarity Association for preserving and encouraging the growth of our apostolate over the course of many years. Without their generous and timely support, this book would not be in your hands.

www.SophiaInstitute.com
www.CatholicExchange.com
www.SophiaInstituteforTeachers.org